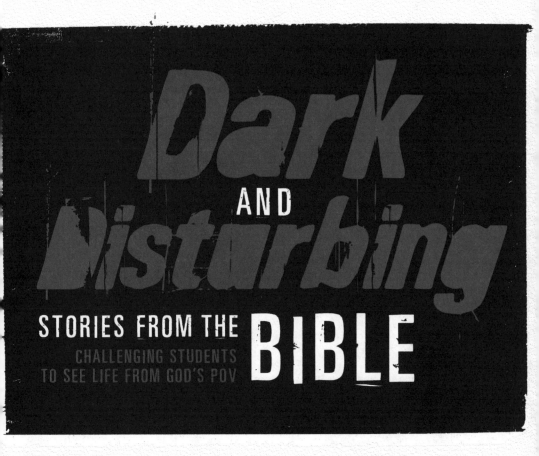

Dark AND Disturbing

STORIES FROM THE BIBLE

CHALLENGING STUDENTS
TO SEE LIFE FROM GOD'S POV

MARY GRACE BECKER & SUSAN MARTINS MILLER

Standard®
PUBLISHING
Bringing The Word to Life
Cincinnati, Ohio

Dark and Disturbing Stories from the Bible

Published by Standard Publishing, Cincinnati, Ohio
www.standardpub.com

Also available: **Shocking and Scandalous Stories from the Bible**, ISBN 978-0-7847-2399-9, Copyright © 2010 Mary Grace Becker and Susan Martins Miller

Printed in: United States of America
Acquisitions editor: Robert Irvin
Project editor: Kelli B. Trujillo
Cover and interior design: Thinkpen Design, Inc., www.thinkpendesign.com

Our thanks for their assistance in the production of the videos for these books goes to: B-Communicated Inc., Cincinnati Christian Schools, Dayton (Ohio) Church of Christ, Hamilton (Ohio) Church of God, LifeSpring Christian Church, Nancy's Hallmark Store (Sharonville, Ohio), TAB Productions, and Bob Wallace.

All Scripture quotations, unless otherwise indicated, are taken from the HOLY BIBLE, NEW INTERNATIONAL VERSION®. NIV®. Copyright © 1973, 1978, 1984 by Biblica, Inc.™ Used by permission of Zondervan. All rights reserved.

Scripture quotations marked (The Message) are taken from THE MESSAGE. Copyright © by Eugene H. Peterson 1993, 1994, 1995, 1996, 2000, 2001, 2002. Used by permission of NavPress Publishing Group.

The content in this book is not reviewed by, licensed by, or affiliated with the Motion Picture Association of America in any way. PG-13 is a registered trademark of the MPAA.

ISBN 978-0-7847-2400-2

15 14 13 12 11 10   1 2 3 4 5 6 7 8 9

Contents

I highly endorse *Dark and Disturbing* and *Shocking and Scandalous Stories from the Bible*. These are comprehensive studies, and anyone, not just middle schoolers, will gain a better grasp of how to present these stories found in the Bible. They're told separately, yet fit together like a scriptural mosaic. The concepts are fabulous. There is no stone unturned, as the books answer questions with candor and yet provide encouragement, hope, and understanding—all while dealing with real-life issues.

— Chris Brownlow, community program coordinator of Colorado Springs, Youth Activities

Mary Grace Becker and Susan Miller beam a spotlight on PG-rated stories in the Bible—stories that portray lust, lawlessness, and violence. Using clear communication and a creative, contemporary format, they grab and hold the interest of middle schoolers. This curriculum equips middle schoolers to resist negative peer pressure and to follow God's prescribed path during a complicated period of life.

— Dr. Jim Dyet, board member and mentor, Jerry Jenkins Christian Writers Guild; retired curriculum editor and pastor

At times it's hard to reach young teens with God's truth because they can portray lack of motivation, disinterest, or boredom with church or spiritual issues. Look no further for the curriculum that will overcome those factors. *Dark and Disturbing* and *Shocking and Scandalous Stories from the Bible* is a powerful, truth-defining, and spiritually challenging curriculum certain to grip the heart of the young teen. A refreshing and thought-provoking delivery of spiritual truths set within the day-to-day tough stuff that young teens face. . . . Awesome!

— Jodi Hoch, middle school teacher and curriculum developer

This is a gem in the middle school curriculum world! Carefully planned lessons allow students to think through their own decisions and actions, connecting spiritual growth to the Bible stories many churches avoid—even though the salacious and disturbing stories of the Bible often attract young teenagers to the honesty and authenticity of Scripture. There is much to be learned in the Bible passages that are difficult and ugly; the authors have gone to tremendous lengths to ensure these lessons hit the issues young teens deal with in creative, entertaining, and respectful ways.

— M. Karen Lichlyter-Klein, pastor, Colorado Springs

Some may find it hard to believe that Mary Grace and Susan are adults! Their uncanny ability to connect with youth brings the Bible alive to a generation that sees it as outdated. As you can see in the faces of the teens in the videos, the core messages fill them with an excitement to dig into God's Word and his plan. If you know teenagers, get these books and check out the curriculum.

— Ron Luce, president, Teen Mania Ministries

For all the youth leaders who asked us for something more. Here it is.

—M.G.B. & S.M.M.

Making the Most of *Dark and Disturbing Stories from the Bible*

Brice and Jason take extreme pleasure in teasing the girls.

Allison craves the attention and often rewards both boys with a friendly slap.

Jordan giggles at everything.

Miranda thinks she's above it all.

Jake refuses to admit he's interested in anything.

Every class discussion carries an undercurrent of wanting to fit in and be noticed.

These lessons are designed to be used in a variety of formats, such as a middle school Sunday school class, a junior high youth group meeting, or even a mid-week small group meeting.

Welcome to middle school! Your students are bursting with independence and often insist on making their own decisions. They are miles away from being elementary-aged kids, but at the same time, too many of them lack the foundation to make wise choices. They want what they value *in the moment,* but don't necessarily consider how it will affect life long-term. What's ethical depends on the situation . . . and what they want out of it. They're fixated on youth culture, media, and technology.

Middle schoolers crave relationships but don't always know how to build positive, supportive friendships. Whether innocent or naïve or just seeking to be different, students in this age group want to fit in *somewhere.* Increasingly, they're swayed by peers and have no fixed reference point to guide their decisions.

This is a tough crowd to lead anywhere—but even a tough crowd needs to hear God's truth. So how do you connect with them and connect them to the truth?

STORIES THAT MAKE GREAT MOVIES

Dark and Disturbing Stories from the Bible emphasizes the authority of God's Word and how middle schoolers can come together to help each other stand strong. It doesn't use the recycled Bible stories kids have heard a bazillion times in Sunday school. Instead, it focuses on stories that leave you asking, "Is that *really* in the Bible?" The stories most curriculums avoid because of their "PG-13" content.

The Motion Picture Association of America describes a PG-13 motion picture as going beyond the PG rating in theme, violence, nudity, sensuality, language, adult activities, or other elements, but not so far that it reaches the restricted

R category. PG-13 movies include some material that may not be suitable for children—and middle schoolers are no longer living in a childlike world.

The stories in *Dark and Disturbing Stories from the Bible*—and our companion volume, *Shocking and Scandalous Stories from the Bible*—will grab the attention of middle schoolers as they're developing values and will get your students to take a close look at moral and ethical issues, and resulting situations, that were relevant in Bible times and still are today. These include things like sexual temptation, popularity, doubts, loneliness and/or depression, greed, and much more. These Bible stories are not about model choices and feel-good moments; instead, most of them are about the *bad* decisions people make. The discussion-based lessons showcase the "me-first" attitude that got many Bible characters into trouble.

Dark and Disturbing Stories from the Bible will give your students the tools they need to make better choices—*godly* choices—when they face PG-13-level challenges in their own lives.

RULES OF ENGAGEMENT

Dark and Disturbing Stories from the Bible is full of opportunities for your students to interact and build strong relationships. They'll connect through dramas, discussions, challenges, group journaling, fun games, and prayer. Through these experiences, they'll discover that they're not alone—they can depend on each other, support each other, and stand strong together against the pressures of peers and culture.

But in order to develop these types of relationships, your meetings need to be a safe environment where participants feel free to express themselves openly without fear of ridicule or rejection. We suggest you establish some "rules of engagement" for your group. A great way to do this is to get the students involved in creating the rules of engagement so that they develop their own expectations for the best ways to interact with each other. Your group's list will be as unique as your students and the realities impacting them.

Here's a sample of what some Rules of Engagement could look like:

Rule #1: God is #1, second to none.

Rule #2: Meetings will begin and end on time. Don't be late!

Rule #3: Cell phones off.

Rule #4: You're important. We want to know what you think and feel.

Rule #5: There are no bad ideas.

Rule #6: What's said and done here stays here.

Rule #7: No complaining—let's find a solution instead.

Another approach is to explore Bible verses and use them as the basis for creating your group's Rules of Engagement. For example, participants could look up verses like these to develop their rules:

Colossians 3:12: Therefore, as God's chosen people, holy and dearly loved, clothe yourselves with compassion, kindness, humility, gentleness and patience. *(Treat each other with respect. We are a team!)*

1 Thessalonians 5:11: Therefore encourage one another and build each other up, just as in fact you are doing. *(Be positive.)*

Proverbs 12:18: Reckless words pierce like a sword, but the tongue of the wise brings healing. *(Think before you blurt something out.)*

Proverbs 18:13: He who answers before listening—that is his folly and his shame. *(Listen without interrupting.)*

Proverbs 8:33: Listen to my instruction and be wise; do not ignore it. *(Take your cues from what the Bible says.)*

Psalm 119:15, 16: I meditate on your precepts and consider your ways. I delight in your decrees; I will not neglect your word. *(Put effort into understanding what the Bible says even if you don't understand it at first.)*

Philippians 2:3: Do nothing out of selfish ambition or vain conceit, but in humility consider others better than yourselves. *(Think about what is good for the others in the class, not just for yourself.)*

As you create your rules together, ask all of your students and leaders to sign or initial the list and display it in your meeting area. This helps create buy-in and will serve as a tangible reminder of the group's commitment to one another.

HOW THESE LESSONS WORK

Teaching a lesson from this book isn't complicated. At the start of each lesson, you'll find a **Director's Commentary**—a section just for you that outlines the key ideas of the lesson and how you'll lead your students in exploring them. First you'll find the Scripture portion the lesson is based on, along with the elements of the story that (we think) qualify it for its "PG-13 rating," a **Key Bible Verse**, and the lesson's **POV** ("point of view"). The POV is the learning focus—the main idea you want your students to take away from their exploration of God's Word. Using student-friendly language, the POV points to God's

Throughout each lesson, you'll see **bolded words**. These are our suggestions of what you can **say** as you're facilitating the lesson and leading discussion. Don't treat these suggestions as a script—be natural as you say them or use your own words to communicate the same idea. You'll also see *italicized* possible answers following some of the discussion questions. These aren't the "right" answers— they're just ideas you can use to help students start talking or to zero in together on the key ideas of the study.

The **dramas** in this book are simple enough that you can select actors and have them read through and act out the skits without advance preparation. But if you've got a group of kids who are really into **acting**, you can recruit them ahead of each lesson and give them opportunities to practice the skits in advance.

perspective and the connection between the Bible passage and students' real lives. You'll also find a simple chart at the beginning of each lesson that outlines what you'll do in each part of the lesson, how long it should take, and what you'll need to pull it off. Finally, to give you extra insight into the biblical content you'll be exploring with your group, you'll find a **Why Is This PG-13 Story in the Bible?** section that provides you with an overview of the Bible story and the ways you can connect it to the lives of your students.

Each lesson is organized into three main parts:

Take 1—Movie Preview

Take 1 begins each lesson with an activity that sets up the day's Bible story in a relational way, such as through dramas, role-plays, icebreaker games, and hands-on projects. Each activity will lead into a lively discussion of modern-day moral or ethical dilemmas that echo the Bible story.

Take 2—Feature Presentation

Take 2 moves your group directly into the Bible story, where students will have a chance to examine the tough choices the people made and the consequences that resulted. Here you'll use an **Outtakes** handout that will help your students get to know the characters **(Cast)**, the story's main points **(Movie Trailer)**, and God's perspective **(POV)** on this situation. Students can read the Scripture passage (from *The Message*) on each **Outtakes** page or they can read it in their own Bibles. Each Take 2 section also includes **Team Talk**—opportunities for participants to look more deeply into the Bible story in a small group setting. (Keep reading for more info on running these small groups.)

Take 3—Critics' Corner

Take 3 will wrap up your lesson by reinforcing the **POV** through reflective discussion, a fun team-building activity, and prayer. The light-hearted team-builder activity at the close of each lesson is a fun, high-energy way to help your students solidify their relationships with each other so that they can support each other in living out the day's POV.

> Add an element of fun to the dramas by stocking a one-size-fits-all **prop box** that your students can use to come up with an instant fun prop, costume, or sound effect for each lesson's drama. A run to a secondhand store or garage sale can yield hats, wigs, scarves, sunglasses, old cell phones, noisemakers, and more.

OUT-OF-THE-BOX WAYS TO CONNECT SCRIPTURE TO LIFE

Along with fun icebreakers, dramas, team-builders, and insightful discussion questions, *Dark and Disturbing Stories from the Bible* uses unique methods like an interactive DVD, group journaling, small group discussion, and teen mentoring to move beyond the typical "listen-to-a-leader-talk" approach to middle school youth meetings or Sunday school classes.

Interactive DVD

Each lesson provides you with an opportunity to connect with your media-savvy students by using a **DVD** to kick-start discussion. In some sessions, the DVD will be an onscreen version of that lesson's skit, so it'll be up to you which avenue you'd prefer. In other sessions, the DVD for that week will use footage of real-life students, just like yours, who are answering questions, doing activities together, or are in hot-seat scenarios. These clips will serve as a catalyst to get your group excited to talk or to prepare them for an activity they're about to do.

In every lesson, the DVD option is meant to enhance and enliven the experience your students are having, so use it as a tool to help keep things exciting. And it may be your choice to do both: have your students act out the drama or answer the questions, then play the DVD. Compare your students to those in our sample video—or better put, let them compare themselves. (Prediction: there's a good chance your students will do some boasting!)

Create a Group Journal

Use a group journal week after week to build community, to allow time for students to reflect, and to create an ongoing record of what students are learning. In each lesson you'll find specific suggestions for things your group can record in its journal, like a question to answer, an idea to brainstorm together, something to sketch, or a choice to evaluate. It's important that you encourage everyone to contribute—it's a *group* journal.

Your group can create a journal in a variety of ways. Here are a few ideas to get you started:

- Use an *oversized newsprint pad.* Decorate the cover with markers and keep the pages in the pad.
- Treat *windows or mirrors* in your meeting area as *dry-erase boards.* Be sure to keep a generous supply of colorful dry-erase markers on hand. (If you use this method, take photos of what the group has written at the end of each study so you have a record of their thoughts.)
- Post *self-stick notes* on the walls. Use a variety of colors and sizes and let students create a fresh, striking visual display each time. (Collect all the notes at the end of each lesson!)
- Set up *large or medium-size white boards/dry-erase boards.* Use one or several so everyone can participate artistically.
- Get creative with *construction paper.* Let your students use paper, scissors, and glue to create pages each week that you can save and bind in an imaginative way.
- Write on pieces of *poster board.* Use various colors and build a big stack each week.
- Compile students' reflections in a *three-ring binder.* Create several pages each week, slip them into sheet protectors, and add them in.
- Make a *scrapbook* together. Get fun papers and other unique scrapbooking supplies, then have participants write directly on the pages or glue in small pieces of colored paper. If you want, add stamps, trims, stickers, and so on.

Team Talk Small Groups

Relationships are the engine that makes these lessons go—that's why each lesson includes a **Team Talk** section in which students can talk openly and candidly in smaller-sized groups. To make these discussion groups the best they can be, aim to have about four to eight students and an adult or older teen leader in each group. When a group is the right size, it will give students (especially the more quiet and introverted ones) an opportunity to open up and dig through the challenges of these Bible stories with others.

Encourage groups to spread out around your meeting area and find their own space to talk. Assign some groups to discuss the first set of questions ("Team Talk 1"), the remaining groups the second set ("Team Talk 2").

In some lessons, you'll see instructions to divide your students into gender-based groups called **Guy Talk** and **Girl Talk**. This occurs when the theme of the story has a sensual element or a clear female perspective. Middle schoolers are ready to wrestle with tough questions, but sometimes they'll feel safer in a just-guys or just-girls group. And, in some cases, it's just best to avoid awkwardness or inappropriate things being said. If your group is too small to divide, handle questions with sensitivity.

Make sure to prep your small group leaders for their role in the Team Talk discussions by having them read the **Why Is This PG-13 Story in the Bible?** section before each lesson to give them extra insight into issues that may come into play during discussions.

Group size: Even if you have only, say, ten participants, it's still important to have students break up into Team Talk small groups. But if you've got just six students or less, it's probably a good idea to have them stay together and discuss both sets of Team Talk questions.

Teen Mentoring

If you can, we strongly recommend that you recruit some mature Christian high school students to help with these lessons. Successful teen mentorship makes a positive difference in the lives of young twelve-, thirteen-, and fourteen-year-olds! Middle schoolers look up to older teens who have successfully navigated the middle school years and are closer to their age than parents and teachers. Likewise, teens learn valuable life skills from leading Bible study discussion among middle schoolers. Mentorship, however, is not for all teens. Teen mentors understand they are role models and leaders-in-training. Mentorship is a responsibility. With that in mind, here are a few things to consider with your teen leaders.

The Power of Parents
Always keep in mind a golden rule for working with middle schoolers: involve their parents and guardians. Welcome parents to drop by and review the curriculum. Ask them to attend from time to time and help with activities. Keep them in the loop! Look for opportunities for hallway conversations, send e-mail or text message updates, and make plenty of phone calls. Build a partnership that surrounds students with God's point of view.

- Be sure to choose godly high schoolers who want to make a difference and who can put the interests of others above their own.
- A successful teen mentor should be someone who's friendly, enthusiastic, insightful, honest, and self-confident. He or she should inspire younger teenagers to be themselves and to rise above negative stereotypes.
- Teen mentors should be responsible and show up each week on time and prepared to lead their Team Talk discussion group.
- Last, mentors should feel free to share personal adolescence stories. Teens who remember what it was like to be a middle schooler will build trust with your students. (However, discussions on dating, high school pranks, or slips in judgment involving sex, smoking, or alcohol and drug use are not appropriate for this age level and should be kept out of the discussion.)

To help your teen mentors be successful in their new roles, be sure to meet with them regularly to pray and talk over lesson points and to get a general feel for how things are going in their Team Talk groups.

READY TO GO!

You have the tools to help your students know God on a deeper level. You have the passion to see it happen. You fully expect that God is going to do something great with your middle schoolers.

So does he. ✖

Director's Commentary

NOW SHOWING: *The Beast Delivers*

FROM THE BIBLE: Balaam encounters power greater than his own (Numbers 22:21-38).

RATED PG-13 FOR: cursing, sorcery, and animal cruelty

POV: When your stubborn ways don't work, give God's way a try.

KEY VERSE: "Show me your ways, O Lord, teach me your paths" (Psalm 25:4).

The Lesson	Time	What you'll do . . .	How you'll do it . . .	What you'll need . . .
Take 1: Preview	15 to 20 minutes	Start off your lesson by introducing the theme with a relational, creative activity.	Option 1: Students perform impromptu role-plays and explore why people blame others.	1 photocopy of the "Blame-storming Session Now in Progress" (p. 23), cut into slips; prop box; group journal supplies, marker (*Optional:* a sweater, science fair sign, softball and bat, printed "minutes" from a student council meeting or facsimile; movie snacks for your audience)
			Option 2: Students watch a DVD version of "Blame-storming Session Now in Progress" and discuss it. Or, choose to do both.	*Dark and Disturbing Stories from the Bible DVD*, TV and DVD player
Take 2: Feature Presentation	15 to 20 minutes	Dive into the Bible story and explore it together.	Small group and large group discussion	Photocopies of **Outtakes** (p. 24); butcher paper or newsprint, markers *Optional:* Bibles
Take 3: Critics' Corner	15 to 20 minutes	Help your students grasp God's point of view and wrap things up with a fun team-building activity.	Discussion, game, and prayer	Group journal; **Outtakes** (p. 24); clean rags or sturdy paper towels (*Optional:* clothespins)

WHY IS THIS PG-13 STORY IN THE BIBLE?

In Numbers 22:1-20, we see that Israel, the new kid on the block when it comes to armies, has become a serious military power. When the Amorite king won't give permission for Israel to pass through his lands peacefully, the Israelites take them by force. Balak, the king of Moab, sits up and pays attention. He thinks he's next in line—although Israel's real target is Jericho. Military strategy does not seem to deter Israel, so Balak decides to hire the famous Balaam to curse Israel and ensure Moab's victory.

Balaam is a prophet for sale. His story breaks up the account of Israel's progress toward the promised land to feature someone who had no faith whatsoever in the one true God. Balaam is an internationally known celebrity spokesman for any god, rather than one who believes in Yahweh. Archaeological evidence dating back to 800 to 700 BC supports his existence and reputation as a "seer," and Scripture mentions him in Numbers, Nehemiah, Micah, 2 Peter, and Revelation. The Bible condemns Balaam in these places for his moral and ethical failings. Typically he would sell his skill and reputation for the right price. Balak, king of Moab, is willing to pay Balaam's price to curse Israel.

Balak sends a delegation to Balaam, who goes through the motions of going off to hear what the Lord has to say—only the Lord really does talk to him! God says not to curse Israel and Balaam declines the job. Balak tries again, and this time God tells Balaam to go—but only say what God wants him to say.

Connecting with Community
Log on to www.darkand disturbing.com to connect with other ministries:
- Check out a sample video of other students in action.
- Share with other leaders at the PG-13 forum about what's working in your ministry, what's not, or how you used *Dark and Disturbing* or *Shocking and Scandalous* this week.
- Or ask for input about other aspects of middle school ministry.

Although he outwardly agrees with these conditions, it's quite possible that Balaam still intends to curse Israel and collect a handsome fee from Balak. So God confronts Balaam on the road to Moab by showing an angel to his donkey (in today's passage, Numbers 22:21-38). The guy with the international reputation is spiritually blind, and a stupid animal sees the truth! To top it off, the donkey talks! Even more, Balaam quickly answers the donkey in his anger, as though they talk with each other every day! It would be comical if not so sad.

When Balaam begins this encounter, he has no clue that the one true God of Israel is in a different class than the supposed gods he's used to dealing with. But when he's confronted by a talking donkey and an angel, Balaam finally understands the power and authority of God. This story will help middle schoolers realize that our stubbornness can never compete with God's power.

Take It to Your Students

Here are some key points to put in front of your students with this lesson:

- Being stubborn can blind you to what's good.
- No matter what we think of ourselves, God is greater.
- Place God above greed. ✗

The Beast Delivers: The Lesson

Take 1: Preview   (15 to 20 minutes)

Setup: This activity will set up the day's Bible story in a relational way as students role-play "blame-storming" situations and explore how stubborn behavior often hides the truth.

Set design: Create a relaxed atmosphere for today's role-plays. Ask students to sit in a circle on pillows, seat cushions, or just on the floor. The performances will be performed in the middle. Popcorn or movie snacks will help set a movie mood.

Makeup and effects: For today's role-plays (and other dramas in this book) consider stocking a one-size-fits-all prop box your students can rummage through to come up with an instant fun prop, costume, or sound effect for the day's drama. A run to secondhand stores or garage sales can yield hats, wigs, scarves, sunglasses, old cell phones, noisemakers, and so on.

Props: Supplies for the journal option you've chosen, markers; 1 photocopy of the "Blame-storming Session Now in Progress" (p. 23), cut into slips; prop box Or play the corresponding clip on the *Dark and Disturbing Stories from the Bible DVD*—or do both.

Optional: a sweater, science fair sign, softball and bat, printed "minutes" from a student council meeting, or facsimile; movie snacks for your audience

QUIET ON THE SET

To launch the lesson:

• Welcome everyone to the group. Use first names or preferred nicknames and introduce visitors. After your students have had some time to socialize, pull them in and have them get comfortable.

> Good idea for a leadership goal: aim to have everybody's name memorized by your next meeting.

• Go over your Rules of Engagement. These class-determined rules help early teens honor each other and give them the freedom to be truthful without ridicule. (See the Rules of Engagement suggestions on p. 6 for more information.)

• Review the journaling component you've chosen for your group. (See Create a Group Journal on p. 10 for more information.)

ACTION

> f you want, make a video of your students' performance of 'Blame-storming Session Now n Progress." Play it back later, perhaps for the entire church!

Option: Show your group "Blame-storming Session Now in Progress" from the *Dark and Disturbing Stories from the Bible DVD* before beginning this activity.

Have students form pairs or trios and explain that they're about to improvise role-play scenarios. They'll pick a "Blame-storming Session Now in Progress" slip, then you'll read it out loud to the whole group. You'll allow the pair or trio about one minute to talk through their ideas, make up their characters, and grab any needed props. After a minute, they'll perform their short improv in front of everybody.

Repeat this process with each pair or trio—allowing just one minute for the students to get ready before they improv in front of everyone. (If you've got more than six pairs or trios, you'll need to repeat some of the scenarios from "Blame-storming Session Now in Progress.")

PLAY BACK

Great performances! Sometimes it seems that the easiest solution to a tough choice is to blame someone else. Being bold for what's right is a good thing. But if our behavior shifts blame and resists responsibility and good advice, well, that's another story.

Spend time reflecting on "Blame-storming Session Now in Progress" with your group by using the discussion questions below. Don't edit your students' responses—allow them to discuss freely. Have a volunteer

> You may want to break into small groups (just guy and girl groups, for instance) for the journaling, discussion, or both.

record the group's impressions in the journaling method you've chosen. Jot "Blame-storming" and today's date at the top of the journal entry. Give every student the opportunity to comment or to journal, even if it's just to initial in agreement with posted entries.

Use these questions to get the discussion going:
- What's the common problem in today's role-plays?
- In your opinion, does stubbornness reflect an open or closed mind? Does it matter? Why or why not?
- Why do you think we so often choose to play the "blame game"?

Great discussion. Today's feature brings a stubbornness to the silver screen. The lead actor digs in his heels—literally—and blames not *someone* but a furry *something* for his outrageous behavior. Today's animal-lovers blockbuster, *The Beast Delivers*, is up next. ✘

Take 2: Feature Presentation   (15 to 20 minutes)

Setup: Your students will take a close look at the story of Balaam's talking donkey and discuss listening to God and his way of doing things.
Props: Photocopies of **Outtakes** (p. 24); butcher paper or newsprint, markers
Optional: Bibles

QUIET ON THE SET

Pass out copies of **Outtakes**, one per student. *Optional:* Have students grab their own Bibles.

ACTION

Use **Outtakes** to introduce and teach the Bible story. First, briefly introduce the **Cast** and make sure your students know who's who. Next, use **Movie Trailer** to briefly cover the highlights of the Bible background and story. Then read the

Bible story (Numbers 22:21-38) aloud from **Outtakes** or have a volunteer read it. If you prefer, ask students to read the passage out loud from their own Bibles.

PLAY BACK

Divide your group into two or more discussion teams with an older teen or adult leader for each group. Assign half the teams to explore the perspectives of Balak and Balaam (Team Talk 1, below) and the other half to explore the perspectives of the donkey and the angel (Team Talk 2). Remind group leaders to be prepared to enhance discussion with insights from **Why Is This PG-13 Story in the Bible?** (p. 14).

> If you've got six students or less, you can discuss all the questions as one group.

Give each group a large piece of butcher paper and markers. Have students discuss and write about the motivations they see in the story characters, using the questions below.

A talking *Equus asinus*? Believe it! Draw the outline of a cartoon-style donkey and write your discussion points inside the lines or as speech balloons as we get inside the heads of the donkey, an angel, a sorcerer, and a king.

Team Talk 1: Get into the heads of Balaam and Balak.

- **What do Balak and Balaam want from each other? Why?** (Balaam gets money. Balak gets his enemy cursed.)
- **How does Balaam's behavior toward the donkey mirror what's in his heart?** (Impatient; beats the donkey. Stubborn; keeps blaming the donkey instead of seeing the truth.)
- **How does God put the squeeze on Balaam? Why do you think God does this?** (The third time the angel appears, Balaam literally is squeezed in between two walls with nowhere to go when the donkey sits down. God is trying to get Balaam to see things his way.)
- **Balaam falls to the ground when he sees the angel. What does he think it means?** (He is finally starting to realize God's power.)

Team Talk 2: Get into the heads of the donkey and the angel.

- What do the donkey and the angel have in common? *(God uses them to send a message.)*
- How does the angel model what Balaam is supposed to do? *(He says what God tells him to say; that's what Balaam is supposed to do.)*
- What do you think it means that God would make a donkey talk to get through to Balaam? *(An animal sees the spiritual truth when Balaam doesn't; maybe Balaam should get a clue. God's power stretches imagination.)*
- We think of a donkey as a stubborn animal. How does the stubborn animal show God's way? *(When she sees the angel, she stops; she knows she can't keep going that way.)*

Bring the discussion teams back together. Briefly review results of discussions by displaying the drawings and reading the discussion notes.

Continue your discussion as a large group by asking questions like:

- In your opinion, what's the big point that Balaam was missing? *(Do things God's way, not your own stubborn way.)*
- Train wreck! What does this story tell us about stubbornness? *(It doesn't get you what's good for you. It ruins relationships. It gets in the way of seeing the truth.)*
- Why do you think this story is in the Bible? *(This is a good opportunity to remind students of the Key Verse, "Show me your ways, O Lord, teach me your paths" [Psalm 25:4].)*

Balaam had legendary status. If he did what Balak wanted and cursed Israel, he'd stand to make very good money.

Use these questions to prompt more large-group discussion:

- Where did Balaam get off the right path? Or was he ever on it?
- How does today's Key Verse show what we can learn from this Bible story?
- Today's POV is: *When your stubborn ways don't work, give God's way a try.* Have you ever given God's way a try in a tough spot? Tell us about it.

Behavior check: Like Balaam, do *you* sometimes refuse to listen because you think you're right? Do you dig in your heels and duck the truth because it may be embarrassing, awkward, or inconvenient? Balaam's is a classic example that when stubborn ways don't work, give God's way a try instead. ✗

Take 3: Critics' Corner   (15 to 20 minutes)

Setup: Reinforce the points you want your students to take away from today's lesson.

Props: Group journal with entries from Take 1; **Outtakes** (p. 24); clean rags or sturdy paper towels, one per student

(*Optional:* clothespins)

QUIET ON THE SET

Grab the group journal and lead students in reviewing the day's earlier blame-storming role-play entries.

ACTION

Consider the POV

Discuss how stubborn behavior can create a false sense of the truth, making problems worse. Examples: shouting "Because I said so!" even when you know you're wrong or saying "Whatever!" to create the impression you know better than the truth.

Invite the group to share some more real-life examples of stubbornness among teens and preteens; add them to the group journal.

Ask the group:

- How do *you* usually respond to stubborn *(or defiant)* behavior by others?
- In what situations do you sometimes react by being stubborn?
- How can stubborn behavior harm God's creation and the creatures that live in it? Explain.
- What positive actions could counteract the blame-storming we role-played earlier? *(Own up to stubborn behavior and move on; practice self-control; be a respectful listener; find the right person to help; commit to break the blame-game habit with God's truths in mind.)*

Draw students' attention to the **POV** on the **Outtakes** handout: *When your stubborn ways don't work, give God's way a try.* Invite students to explain this idea in their own words.

Understand God's Truth

Balaam's "curse work" was known the world over. True to form, his outsized personality was used to getting what it wanted. Stubborn behavior, however, is no match for God's directions. God knows more than we do.

Ask the group:

• **What have you learned from today's story?** *(A stubborn and spiritually blind prophet is no match for the one true God.)*

I don't want you to answer out loud, but I want you to think about this. Grade your behavior this week. Pass? Fail? Great? Poor? How does your own stubborn behavior put distance between you and God's truths? (Allow students a few moments to think about this on their own.) **If you didn't have such a great week, be thinking of ways you can do better.**

Lesson learned: Want to get on the Creator's nerves? Be an obstinate prophet-for-hire who repeatedly beats a defenseless donkey that is simply trying to talk some God-sense into him. Hmm. And they call donkeys stubborn!

Teamwork

Stubbornness can destroy friendships. On the other hand, when we choose to follow God's way, we act with gentleness, grace, intelligence, self-control, and good will toward others. As we seek to follow Jesus, our friendships grow stronger and stronger.

PLAY BACK

Wrap up the meeting with an activity that helps students reflect on giving God's way a try in a stubbornly sinful world. Then close in prayer.

Tail Spin

Needed: clean rags or sturdy paper towels, one for each player
(*Optional:* clothespins)
Goal: Scramble to safety from "Balaams" who are out to get you.

How to Play:

Have everyone pretend to be a donkey. (Hang in there! This game is more fun than that opening line sounds!) Give each player a rag for a tail, tucked into a back pocket or waistband. Have all "donkeys" form a circle. Tell players that each of them must look around the circle and secretly (only to themselves) pick another person to be Balaam (the bad guy). Do not tell anyone. It's a secret! Players must then secretly choose another person from the circle to be the Donkey Rescuer (the good guy). No one knows who is who.

Option: For a rowdy part two to your game time, have players form human chains, placing hands on the waists of those in front. Chains or "donkey caravans" must run to capture the tails—this time, they are clothespins—from other caravans. Of course, caravans must do all they can to protect their own clothespin tails! No taking hands off the person in front; doing so eliminates that donkey caravan from the game.

The Verse-atility option is a middle school-friendly, personalized rewording of the Key Verse. Use it to help your students really get what the Key Verse is all about.

Verse-atility: Father, teach me the right way.

On the count of three, "donkeys" (everyone) must run for their furry lives away from the Balaam they've each selected while seeking protection behind their secret Donkey Rescuer. Because no one knows who anyone else has picked, chaos will result!

Be prepared for a lot of running and evading. Players seeking the protection of a Donkey Rescuer may be seen by that player as a nasty Balaam! If there's time, have students play two or three more rounds of this game, mentally selecting different Balaams and Donkey Rescuers each time.

Afterward, say: **A stubbornly sinful world results in chaos nearly all the time. Instead, let's make things easier on each other. Let's choose to live by God's Spirit through positive action. Be an inspiration to others.**

Close with Prayer

To keep God's truth front and center in your students' lives, ask your group to look again at **Outtakes** and repeat today's **Key Verse**: "Show me your ways, O Lord, teach me your paths" (Psalm 25:4). Also point out this week's *Verse-atility*, a personalized wording of today's Key Verse: *Father, teach me the right way.* If time permits, jot the verse in the group journal and have everyone initial it.

Invite students to share prayer requests, especially those that connect to the main ideas of the lesson. In prayers, ask God to show the specific paths he wants for each of your students, whether big situations or the daily ones. ✘

DRESS CODE

Role-play: Shawna stubbornly refuses to admit she borrowed her sister's sweater without asking permission.

✂ --

ON THE FLY

Role-play: Greg forgot to complete his assignment for the team's insect science fair project. The others have done their work. Faced with a failing grade, Greg looks for someone or something to blame.

✂ --

STRIKE ZONE

Role-play: Five straight losses certify the Wild Cats as losers! At least, that's how the star pitcher sees it. He or she blames the team's poor hitting and fielding for the Cats' terrible stats.

✂ --

HARD DRIVE

Role-play: The student council secretary insists that he or she sent every council member the minutes from last month's meeting. No one has seen the report. With time running out, the secretary can only think of one thing: he or she threatens to cancel the spring dance.

✂ --

A FREE RIDE

Role-play: Craig's bored. Just for fun, Craig and Carl decide to let the air out of the bus tires at school. When certain they've been caught on security cameras, Carl thumbs to Craig and shouts, "It was all his idea!"

✂ --

NOT-SO-SWEET

Role-play: Connie and Lynn had a blast at the candy factory tour. Afterward, with no one looking, Lynn slips a few things from the factory's gift shop into her purse. "Go for it," Connie urges Lynn. "These gift shops charge too much anyway."

Outtakes

CAST

Balaam: a famous sorcerer—not one of God's people
Balak: king of Moab
Donkey: Balaam's faithful service animal
God's Angel

MOVIE TRAILER

- The people of Moab are afraid of Israel's army that's camped and ready to attack.
- Moab's King Balak decides to hire Balaam to curse Israel.
- Balaam travels to see Balak, but his donkey sees an angel of the Lord and stops three times.
- Tired of being beaten, the donkey talks! God tells Balaam to only say what God says.
- Balak is angry that Balaam didn't come faster.
- Instead of cursing Israel, Balaam blesses Israel.

Verse-atility: Father, teach me the right way.

POV: When your stubborn ways don't work, give God's way a try.
Key Verse: "Show me your ways, O Lord, teach me your paths" (Psalm 25:4).

THE BEAST DELIVERS Numbers 22:21-38 (The Message) (We've added a few of our own comments in **bold** below.)

[Prologue: Balaam was internationally known for his power to curse. Balak, king of Moab, wanted to hire Balaam to curse Israel. He sent men to get Balaam. Balaam had to travel a long way to do this job.]

Balaam got up in the morning, saddled his donkey, and went off with the noblemen from Moab. As he was going, though, God's anger flared. The angel of God stood in the road to block his way. Balaam was riding his donkey, accompanied by his two servants. When the donkey saw the angel blocking the road and brandishing a sword, she veered off the road into the ditch. Balaam beat the donkey and got her back on the road. **[A hit and run!]**

But as they were going through a vineyard, with a fence on either side, the donkey again saw God's angel blocking the way and veered into the fence, crushing Balaam's foot against the fence. Balaam hit her again. **[Stop that!]**

God's angel blocked the way yet again—a very narrow passage this time; there was no getting through on the right or left. Seeing the angel, Balaam's donkey sat down under him. Balaam lost his temper; he beat the donkey with his stick.

Then God gave speech to the donkey. She said to Balaam: "What have I ever done to you that you have beat me these three times?"

Balaam said, "Because you've been playing games with me! If I had a sword I would have killed you by now." **[Uh . . . talking don-key?!]**

The donkey said to Balaam, "Am I not your trusty donkey on whom you've ridden for years right up until now? Have I ever done anything like this to you before? Have I?"

He said, "No."

Then God helped Balaam see what was going on: He saw God's angel blocking the way, brandishing a sword. Balaam fell to the ground, his face in the dirt.

God's angel said to him: "Why have you beaten your poor donkey these three times? I have come here to block your way because you're getting way ahead of yourself. The donkey saw me and turned away from me these three times. If she hadn't, I would have killed you by this time, but not the donkey. I would have let her off." **[Angel avenger and animal lover.]**

Balaam said to God's angel, "I have sinned. I had no idea you were standing in the road blocking my way. If you don't like what I'm doing, I'll head back."

But God's angel said to Balaam, "Go ahead and go with them. But only say what I tell you to say— absolutely no other word."

And so Balaam continued to go with Balak's nobles.

When Balak heard that Balaam was coming, he went out to meet him in the Moabite town that was on the banks of the Arnon, right on the boundary of his land.

Balak said to Balaam, "Didn't I send an urgent message for help? Why didn't you come when I called? Do you think I can't pay you enough?"

Balaam said to Balak, "Well, I'm here now. But I can't tell you just anything. I can speak only words that God gives me—no others." **[I've seen the light!]**

[Epilogue: Balaam blessed Israel. But later Balak's people convinced Israel to worship a false god.]

Director's Commentary

NOW SHOWING: *Star-struck*

FROM THE BIBLE: The sun stands still (Joshua 10:1-15).

RATED PG-13 FOR: disturbing images (death by hailstones)

POV: Don't give up the chance to be bold for God.

KEY VERSE: "Since we have such a hope, we are very bold" (2 Corinthians 3:12).

The Lesson	Time	What you'll do . . .	How you'll do it . . .	What you'll need . . .
Take 1: Preview	15 to 20 minutes	Start off your lesson by introducing the theme with a relational, creative activity.	Option 1: Students make a bold statement by creating personal trademarks.	Pencils and paper; group journal supplies, marker; examples of trademark symbols from magazines, packaging, or the Internet; glue, tape, or paper clips
			Option 2: Students watch a DVD version of "Standout" and discuss their own views on standing out from the crowd. Or, choose to do both.	*Dark and Disturbing Stories from the Bible* DVD, TV and DVD player
Take 2: Feature Presentation	15 to 20 minutes	Dive into the Bible story and explore it together.	Small group and large group discussion	Photocopies of **Outtakes** (p. 36); newsprint sheets or pieces of poster boards, markers
Take 3: Critics' Corner	15 to 20 minutes	Help your students grasp God's point of view and wrap things up with a fun team-building activity.	Discussion, game, and prayer	Photocopies of **Outtakes** (p. 36); group journal supplies; video camera and 1 photo-copy of the "Bold Words for God Cards" handout (p. 35), cut apart

WHY IS THIS PG-13 STORY IN THE BIBLE?

Israel is on the march: the walls of Jericho have tumbled (Joshua 6), Ai is destroyed (Joshua 8), Gibeon has surrendered (Joshua 9). Israel is now well established as a military force. Five kings decide they don't like this, not one bit, and they band together to go on the offensive. They refuse to just sit and wait for these invaders to show up.

When news spreads that the five kings are advancing, Joshua's army marches all night to the battle zone on a strategic trade route. The low-lying hills between the coast to the west and the higher lands to the east are critical territory to control travel and commerce. Joshua approaches the confrontation with an assurance of victory from God (10:8), but does that mean there won't be bloodshed?

This battle is as unconventional as the famous fall of Jericho. In the early morning hours, Joshua surprises the armies of the five kings. God throws the enemy into confusion, so they turn and run, and for good measure God sends a deadly hailstorm. But there are five armies to rout, and Joshua apparently decides Israel could use a little extra time to get the job done.

He boldly prays for the sun to stand still.

The traditional explanation is that God stopped the rotation of the earth so the sun did in fact stand still that day, giving Israel some extra daylight hours for the battle. Other scholars read the passage figuratively, or as poetry, or translate the words to mean simply that the weather became cooler or the sky was overcast, seeming to extend the part of the day when fighting would be likely.

Whatever happened that day, it was memorable. It's recorded in the Book of Jashar, an early account of Israel's wars well known in ancient Israel (10:13), and verse 14 says there has never been another day like this one, either before or since. While we might not know the science of what happened, we know the day involved divine intervention worth remembering. God heard Joshua's

---

Connecting with Community

Log on to www.darkand disturbing.com to connect with other ministries:

- Check out a sample video of other students in action.
- Share with other leaders at the PG-13 forum about what's working in your ministry, what's not, or how you used *Dark and Disturbing* or *Shocking and Scandalous* this week.
- Or ask for input about other aspects of middle school ministry.

bold prayer and gave Israel a miraculous defeat that advanced its position in the land God promised to give his chosen people.

This story will help middle school students see that God works in unexpected ways. He welcomes bold prayers.

Take It to Your Students

Here are some key points to put in front of your students with this lesson:

- Don't underestimate the ways God can choose to work.
- God welcomes our bold requests.
- Don't miss out on the chance to be bold for God. ✗

Star-struck: The Lesson

Take 1: Preview (15 to 20 minutes)

Setup: This activity will set up the day's Bible story in a relational way as students create a personalized trademark and discuss what it means to make a bold mark on the world.

Props: Pencils and paper; group journal supplies, marker; examples of trademark symbols from magazines, packaging, or the Internet; glue, tape or paper clips

Or play the corresponding clip on the *Dark and Disturbing Stories from the Bible DVD*—or do both activities.

QUIET ON THE SET

To launch the lesson:

- Welcome everyone to the group. Use first names or preferred nicknames and introduce visitors. After your students have had some time to socialize, pull them in and have them get comfortable.
- Go over your Rules of Engagement. (See the Rules of Engagement suggestions on p. 6 for more information.)
- Review the journaling method you've chosen for your group. (See Create a Group Journal on p. 10 for more information.)

Option: Have students try some of these other options for making their trademarks: Twist chenille wires around their fingers to create colorful trademark symbols. Or for cool 3-D geometric shapes, cut drinking straws in half. Take paper clips and open them slightly. Insert the rounded ends into separate straws to form "elbow" fasteners. Build your shape.

ACTION

Set out pencils and paper for sketching, then show the group several examples of trademark symbols that you found.

A trademark is a bold symbol that identifies a company and its product. Apple, Disney, and Google are trademark names. The Nike swoosh and McDonald's Golden Arches are examples of famous trademark symbols. I'd like you to create a trademark symbol or logo that boldly tells the world who *you* are.

Have students sketch their trademark ideas. Simple trademark designs can be initials, geometric shapes, a cross, heart, people, animals, and so on. Have students look at the examples you've brought to get their creative wheels turning.

When they're done, add all the finished sketches (with names) to the group journal. Jot "My Mark on the World!" and today's date at the top of the journal entry.

PLAY BACK

Spend time viewing the group's unique trademarks. Ask the group:

• What does your trademark say about you?

• What bold statement do you want to make to the world?

Your trademarks show creativity and passion. Ready to *really* go bold? What if we were to print them on T-shirts or showcase them on a social networking Web site? A trademark bears witness to a belief, a set of ideals, a mission. Trademarks are not mediocre, wishy-washy, ho-hum doodles. They represent a commitment and a promise. When I look at your designs, I see "you" and your willingness to put yourself out there. The image you create is bold and confident.

DVD Option: Play the "Standout" video on the *Dark and Disturbing Stories from the Bible DVD* to kick-start your group's discussion of the next few questions, or do the activity and play the video. After the video, ask your students:

• Who's your biggest role model? Why?

• What do you think it means to stand out from the crowd—to be a "standout"?

• What's one way a Christian teenager could—or should—stand out from the crowd?

• Are you a standout? Name a courageous act you've performed recently.

- How willing (or able) are you to stand tall for yourself and others, even when it means putting up with social ridicule?

Today's highly anticipated cinematic hero is bold on an epic scale. What he asks of his God is ginormous! And God's response? Well, let's just say it hasn't been seen before or since. (That's what the Bible says in Joshua 10!) The stars come out to shine—or do they?—in this week's heart-stopping hit, *Star-struck.*

Take 2: Feature Presentation   (15 to 20 minutes)

Setup: Your students will take a close look at the story of the day the sun stood still and will discuss being bold for God.

Props: Photocopies of **Outtakes** (p. 36); newsprint sheets or pieces of poster board, markers

Optional: Bibles

QUIET ON THE SET

Pass out copies of **Outtakes** (p. 36), one per student. *Optional:* Have students grab their own Bibles.

ACTION

Use **Outtakes** to introduce and teach the Bible story. First, briefly introduce the **Cast** and make sure your students know who's who. Next, use **Movie Trailer** to briefly cover the highlights of the Bible background and story. Then read the Bible story (Joshua 10:1-15) out loud from **Outtakes** or have a volunteer read it. If you prefer, ask students to read the passage aloud from their own Bibles.

PLAY BACK

Divide your group into two or more small teams for discussion with an older teen or adult leader for each group. Assign half the teams to explore the actions of the five kings (Team Talk 1, below) and the other half to explore Joshua's motivations and actions (Team Talk 2). Remind group leaders to be prepared to enhance discussion with insights from **Why Is This PG-13 Story in the Bible?** (p. 26).

Give each discussion team a newsprint sheet or piece of poster board and marker. Assign some teams to draw a crescent moon shape (for the five kings) and the others to draw a sun shape (for Joshua). As students discuss the questions below, they can write about the motivations they see in the story characters inside their shape.

So five kings gang up on Joshua and his army, but the plan backfires. Let's get an insider's look at what led to this surprising battle.

Team Talk 1: Get into the heads of the five kings.

- Why do you think the kings agreed to gang up together? *(Israel was having military success. Gibeon was on Israel's side now.)*
- What do you think the kings thought when the hail started to fall? When the sun stood still? What would you have thought or felt if you were in their shoes?
- What's the difference between the kind of boldness the kings showed and Joshua's bold prayer? *(The kings were trying to establish their own power. Joshua asked for something only God could do.)*
- What lesson could the kings learn from this battle?

Team Talk 2: Get into the head of Joshua.

- How does Joshua respond to Gibeon's plea for help? *(He immediately takes an army and goes.)*
- Since Joshua was already winning the battle, why would he boldly pray for more daylight? *(He prayed for something only God could do; God's power would be displayed.)*
- What do you think gave Joshua the guts to pray for something so outrageous? Explain. *(God has already promised the victory.)*
- How would you describe Joshua's attitude toward the impossible?

Bring the discussion teams back together. Briefly review results of discussions by reviewing the notes written in the moon and sun shapes.

Continue your discussion as a large group by asking questions like:

- How did God show who's who in this story?
- Do you think Joshua told God what to do? Explain.
- Why do you think this story is in the Bible? *(This is a good opportunity to remind students of the Key Verse: "Since we have such a hope, we are very bold" [2 Corinthians 3:12].)*

Let's review what Joshua knows. He *knows* that God has promised his people the land. He *knows* he's already had several stunning military victories because

of what God has done. *He knows* God has guaranteed victory in this present battle. Faith plus assurance creates opportunity and makes for a very bold Joshua.

Use these questions to prompt more large-group discussion:

- What choices could the characters in this story have made that might have changed the story? *(If the kings had not attacked, the battle wouldn't have happened. Joshua could have chosen not to pray boldly for the sun to stop.)*
- How does today's Bible verse illustrate the point of the story?
- Bad things don't always happen to somebody else. Still, God is in your corner. What does this story have to do with being hopeful in your life?

We might not understand the science of what happened that day, but we know God responded on a cosmic scale—hugely, incredibly, and fantastically so. Don't miss the chance to be bold for God. He desires your commitment—your willingness to be an ally. Ultimately, how he responds to your bold request is up to him. ✘

> If your students have difficulty understanding the meaning of Joshua 10:14, help them understand that God was already at work bringing victory to the Israelites. Joshua's request expressed his willingness to put himself out there and be part of God's righteous action plan. God responded to his bold request of faith.

Take 3: Critics' Corner (15 to 20 minutes)

Setup: Reinforce the points you want your students to take away from today's lesson.
Props: Group journal with trademark symbols attached from Take 1; **Outtakes** (p. 36); video camera, 1 photocopy of the "Bold Words for God Cards" handout (p. 35), cut apart
(Optional: 10 to 15 pairs of sunglasses)

QUIET ON THE SET

Grab the group journal and ask students to look over their trademark symbols. If they wish, have students tweak or embolden their trademark sketches.

ACTION

Consider the POV

Bold action takes confidence.

Have students brainstorm confidence-building tips that would work well for middle schoolers. Tips can include ideas like asking family and friends to express what they admire most about them, making a checklist of attainable goals and acting on that list, wearing their trademarks with confidence, and more.

Draw students' attention to the **POV** on the **Outtakes** page: *Don't give up the chance to be bold for God.* Follow up by brainstorming together ways your group can use their God-given gifts to worship and honor him. Students may come up with ideas like verbalizing their faith to others; volunteering for food drives, lock-ins, or city youth or park programs; going on mission trips; practicing positive Christlike actions with an older teen mentor; and praying boldly. (Depending on how many students you have, you may want to break into smaller groups for this discussion.)

Understand God's Truth

This will be a change of thinking for many of us, but try asking God this week for those things that matter most to *him*. Put him front and center. Then pray boldly for the courage to do his will to make them happen.

Ask the group:

- **What have we learned from today's story?** (*God heard Joshua's prayer and gave Israel a miraculous victory that advanced its position.*)
- **God welcomes bold prayers. Now that you know, what will you pray for?**

God stopped the rotation of the earth at Joshua's request. God is the supreme commander of the universe! And he also loves and cares for each of us.

Whatever God's methods, his heart remains the same: to be present and available for those he loves.

Teamwork

Check the scorecard. Throughout the Bible, God acts in ways beyond human imagination. Creation blossoms. The sea divides. The sun stands still. God's Son walks the earth. The dead are raised. Such amazing things *can* be disturbing to those who don't know or honor God.

As we support and encourage each other through words and actions, we can live in a bold and confident faith. Let's step up and unfold God's bold plan this week.

PLAY BACK

Wrap up the meeting with a team-building activity that will help students practice confidence. Then close in prayer.

Bold Talent!

Needed: Video camera; 1 copy of the "Bold Words for God Cards" handout (p. 35), cut apart (*Optional:* sunglasses to share among performing groups)

Goal: Work together to create a unique video.

How to Play:

Make a "Bold Talent!" video with your students. First, separate students into girl and guy groups of any size. (Mixed teams are OK too.) Have teams each pick a choreographer, then hand each choreographer a "Bold Words for God" card. Ask choreographers to come up with a 30-second motion-and-rhythm routine that best demonstrates the word on the card and teach it to his or her group to perform in unison. Prompt choreographers to incorporate bold movements into their routines, like foot stomps, leg slaps, finger snaps, fist punches in the air, rhythmic claps, crisp head action, robotic sequences, and waist twists.

> **Option:** Have groups include POV cheer chants in their performances: *Don't give up the chance to be bold for God!*

> **Option:** Instead of choreography, try it this way. Challenge teams to come up with a silent, 30-seconds-or-less skit that depicts the word on their card. Then, one group at a time, teams act out their skit while other teams guess. After each skit, the team can repeat: "I live for God. Label me _____ (bold word)!"

As a way of introduction and to encourage audience participation, have groups begin each performance with a "Bold Word" card sound off. For example, the team with the "Proud" card will shout, "Give me a p-r-o-u-d for God. What's that spell? PROUD!" Teams then launch into their routines. (Have kids slip on sunglasses to heighten the cool factor!) Lead the other groups in applause for each team and use a video camera to record all performances. (They'll be terrific!)

After all the teams present their bold word, say something like: **Sudden impact! It's not hard to be bold for God if we are in step and have great backup. Ready to boldly go where you've never gone before? Good. Go spread the Word.**

Close with Prayer

Ask your group to look again at **Outtakes** and repeat today's **Key Verse:** "Since we have such a hope, we are very bold" (2 Corinthians 3:12). Then point out

Verse-atility: *Got hope? Be bold for Christ!*

the friendly *Verse-atility* saying: *Got hope? Be bold for Christ!* If time permits, jot the verse in the group journal and have everyone initial around it.

Remind students of Joshua 10:14: "There's never been a day like that before or since—God took orders from a human voice!" *(The Message)*. Invite students to share prayer requests, especially bold ones that show they want to be part of God's work. Emphasize that we never know how God might choose to work. Pray boldly! ✖

CONFIDENT

COURAGEOUS

PROUD

Outstanding

Inspired

Outtakes

CAST

Joshua: leader of Israel
Gibeon: people conquered by Israel
Adoni-Zedek: (aka My-Master-Zedek) king of Jerusalem, afraid of Israel
Four kings of the Amorites: allies to Adoni-Zedek

MOVIE TRAILER

- Israel has been winning battles and making other nations afraid. The emerging nation has just conquered Gibeon.
- Adoni-Zedek, king of Jerusalem, asks four other kings to help him attack Gibeon.
- Joshua takes an army and goes to defend Gibeon.
- Israel chases the enemy. God sends a hailstorm to wipe out the enemy.
- Joshua asks God to make the sun stand still while they fight.
- The sun stops in its tracks for a whole day.

Verse-atility: Got hope? Be bold for Christ.

POV: Don't give up the chance to be bold for God.
Key Verse: "Since we have such a hope, we are very bold" (2 Corinthians 3:12).

STAR-STRUCK Joshua 10:1-15 *(The Message)*

*(We've added a few of our own comments in **bold** below.)*

It wasn't long before My-Master-Zedek king of Jerusalem heard that Joshua had taken Ai and destroyed it and its king under a holy curse, just as he had done to Jericho and its king. He also learned that the people of Gibeon had come to terms with Israel and were living as neighbors. He and his people were alarmed: Gibeon was a big city—as big as any with a king and bigger than Ai—and all its men were seasoned **[lethal]** fighters.

Adoni-Zedek king of Jerusalem sent word to Hoham king of Hebron, Piram king of Jarmuth, Japhia king of Lachish, and Debir king of Eglon: "Come and help me. Let's attack Gibeon; they've joined up with Joshua and the People of Israel."

So the five Amorite (Western) kings—the king of Jerusalem, the king of Hebron, the king of Jarmuth, the king of Lachish, and the king of Eglon—combined their armies and set out to attack Gibeon.

The men of Gibeon sent word to Joshua camped at Gilgal, "Don't let us down now! Come up here quickly! Save us! Help us! All the Amorite kings who live up in the hills have ganged up on us." **[Kings ready to rumble . . .]**

So Joshua set out from Gilgal, his whole army with him—all those tough soldiers! God told him, "Don't give them a second thought. I've put them under your thumb—not one of them will stand up to you."

Joshua **[road warrior]** marched all night from Gilgal and took them by total surprise. God threw them into total confusion before Israel, a major victory at Gibeon. Israel chased them along the ridge to Beth Horon and fought them all the way down to Azekah and Makkedah. As they ran from the People of Israel, down from the Beth Horon ridge and all the way to Azekah, God pitched huge stones on them out of the sky and many died. More died from the hailstones **[ice wars!]** than the People of Israel killed with the sword.

The day God gave the Amorites up to Israel, Joshua spoke to God, with all Israel listening **[how *bold* is that?]**:

"Stop, Sun, over Gibeon;
Halt, Moon, over Aijalon Valley."
And Sun stopped,
Moon stood stock still
Until he defeated his enemies.

(You can find this written in the Book of Jashar.) The sun stopped in its tracks in mid sky; just sat there all day. **[Uh-huh, that's what it says.]** There's never been a day like that before or since—God took orders from a human voice! Truly, God fought for Israel.

Then Joshua returned, all Israel with him, to the camp at Gilgal.

Deadly Force

Director's Commentary

NOW SHOWING: *Deadly Force*

FROM THE BIBLE: Ehud kills Eglon, king of Moab (Judges 3:12-30).

RATED PG-13 FOR: assassination

POV: Don't underestimate the power of one.

KEY VERSE: "He will call upon me, and I will answer him; I will be with him in trouble, I will deliver him and honor him" (Psalm 91:15).

The Lesson	Time	What you'll do . . .	How you'll do it . . .	What you'll need . . .
Take 1: Preview	15 to 20 minutes	Start off your lesson by introducing the theme with a relational, creative activity.	Option 1: Students act out "The Power of One" drama and discuss it.	2 copies of the "The Power of One" (pp. 47, 48); group journal supplies, markers (*Optional:* items from your prop box; TV, remote control, two chairs or maybe comfy bean bag chairs for sitting, business class "assignment sheet" for the actors)
			Option 2: Students watch a DVD version of "The Power of One." Or, choose to do both.	*Dark and Disturbing Stories from the Bible DVD*, TV and DVD player; markers, group journal supplies
Take 2: Feature Presentation	15 to 20 minutes	Dive into the Bible story and explore it together.	Small group and large group discussion	Photocopies of **Outtakes** (p. 49); cards prominently displaying a "1" *Optional:* Bibles, paper, and pens
Take 3: Critics' Corner	15 to 20 minutes	Help your students grasp God's point of view and wrap things up with a fun team-building activity.	Discussion, game, and prayer	Photocopies of **Outtakes** (p. 49); group journal; box of toothpicks, empty 20-ounce plastic drink bottles, tape or string

WHY IS THIS PG-13 STORY IN THE BIBLE?

Once Israel was in the promised land, everything should have been oh-so-sweet, right? Not so much. The book of Judges describes life in Israel from the death of Joshua—who'd led them in conquering the land—up until Israel's first king. During this span of time, judges led the people and dispensed justice. It became easy for the Israelites to get used to being on their own rather than depending on God. They wandered away from God, which prompted God to discipline them and refocus their attention by periodically allowing a foreign king to take over.

Several kings invaded Israel during the time of the judges, including Eglon, king of Moab. For most of two decades, Eglon reminds Israel who's boss, until a guy named Ehud decides enough is enough. We're told that Ehud is left-handed, something we might not pay a lot of attention to—but it's a trait that's important to the story.

The Israelites send Ehud with a tribute payment—a tax that's a sign of submission. Without the tribute, the oppressing king might make the people's lives even more miserable. This time, however, Ehud carries more than just the tribute. After he presents the payment, he asks for a private conference. Everyone else clears out of the room and Ehud pulls out his secret weapon—literally. He has a sword strapped to his right thigh. Because he's left-handed, he can pull the sword from an unexpected location. Acting alone and using his own wits, he kills the king. Ehud sneaks out before anyone realizes what he's done. (Eglon's unsuspecting guards think the king is using the toilet.) On Ehud's signal, Israel attacks and reestablishes its independence for the next eighty years, with Ehud as its leader.

Ehud's story is the first of several cycles in the book of Judges in which Israel turns away from God, becomes oppressed by a foreign leader, cries out to God, and finally is delivered by a person God raises up for that purpose. The nation certainly makes its share of mistakes, but every time, God responds to their repentance.

This story will help middle schoolers realize they can put their individual traits in God's hands. And that even in a tough situation, God can do something great.

Take It to Your Students

Here are some key points to put in front of your students with this lesson:

- When you call on God, he hears you.
- When you answer God's call, he sticks with you.
- One person can make a difference. ✗

Deadly Force: The Lesson

Take 1: Preview (15 to 20 minutes)

Setup: This activity will set up the day's Bible story in a relational way as your group watches how a school assignment brings individual strengths to light.

Set design: Create a relaxed atmosphere for this section of the lesson. Ask students to sit on the floor in a circle on pillows, seat cushions, or colorful mats. The drama will be performed in the middle. Popcorn or movie snacks will help set a movie mood.

Makeup and effects: For today's drama, consider having students select props and costumes from your one-size-fits-all prop box.

Props: Supplies for the journal option you've chosen, markers; 2 copies of the "The Power of One" skit (pp. 47, 48); or the *Dark and Disturbing Stories from the Bible DVD* and a TV with DVD player—or do both activities (*Optional:* items from your prop box; TV, remote control, two chairs or comfy bean bag chairs for sitting, business class "assignment sheet" for the actors)

QUIET ON THE SET

To launch the lesson:

- Welcome everyone to the group. Use first names or preferred nicknames and introduce visitors. After your students have had some time to socialize, pull them in and have them get comfortable while sitting in a circle.

- Go over your Rules of Engagement, if necessary. (See the Rules of Engagement suggestions on p. 6 for more information.)
- Review the journaling component you've chosen for your group. (See Create a Group Journal on p. 10 for more information.)

Option: If you want, make a video of your students' performance of "The Power of One." Play it back later, for the group, the group and parents, or perhaps the entire church.

Just a reminder that the **bold texts** in these lessons are suggestions for what you can **say** as you teach. Remember that this isn't a script; always feel free to take our ideas and put them in your own words.

ACTION

Either have students perform "The Power of One" skit, watch "The Power of One" on the *Dark and Disturbing Stories from the Bible DVD*, or do both. If you choose to have students perform the skit live, give copies of "The Power of One" handout to the student actors and have them prep by reading through their parts a time or two. Also, invite actors to rummage through the prop box for items to enhance the performance.

PLAY BACK

Spend time reflecting on "The Power of One" with your group by using the discussion suggestions below. Don't edit your students' responses—allow them to discuss freely. Have a volunteer record the group's thoughts and impressions in the group journal. Jot "Success Story" and today's date at the top of the journal entry. Give every student the opportunity to comment or to journal, even if it's just to enter their initials in agreement with posted entries.

Having what it takes—when it really counts—puts the "power of one" into play.

Use these questions to get group discussion going:

- What's the main concern in today's skit?
- Have you ever felt empowered (successful or confident) completing a hard task? Describe what you did.
- What do you feel the most empowered doing? The least?
- Do you know any heroes? Describe what it must feel like to be a hero.

The idea that individuals can be called on to get the job done empowers them to use their skills to the max.

In today's rated PG-13 scene, our lead actor has had enough. He's had it with the overtaxing fat cat that now rules his and his neighbors' world. He single-handedly strikes at oppression's heart. Stealth plus a quick getaway in *Deadly Force*, up next.

Take 2: Feature Presentation (15 to 20 minutes)

Setup: Your students will take a close look at the story of Ehud and discuss answering God's call in critical moments.

Props: Photocopies of **Outtakes** (p. 49); cards displaying a prominent "1" (enough for one for each small group, see more below)

Optional: Bibles, paper, and pen

QUIET ON THE SET

Pass out copies of **Outtakes**, one per student. Optional: Have students grab their own Bibles.

ACTION

Use **Outtakes** to introduce and teach the Bible story. First, briefly introduce the **Cast** and make sure your students know who's who. Next, use **Movie Trailer** to cover the highlights of the Bible background and story. Then read the Bible story (Judges 3:12-30) aloud from **Outtakes** or have a volunteer read it. If you prefer, ask students to read the passage from their Bibles.

PLAY BACK

Divide your group into small teams for discussion with an older teen or adult leader for each group. Assign about half the teams to explore the actions and choices of Ehud (Team Talk 1, below) and the other half to look at the actions of Eglon and his servants (Team Talk 2).

The bathroom reference and remark about the king's obesity in today's story are real-life details and don't need to be hidden. Some of your students may find them pretty funny. But those things said, it's important to be careful not to let natural laughter distract from the main point of the story and to be sure not to let students make a big deal about Eglon's size, thus possibly hurting the feelings of other students who struggle with their weight. Tell your class that people in the Bible are not fictional characters but real people with real needs. If necessary, expand the conversation to say that body size is what it is, but does not define a person. Then redirect discussion to the main points.

Remind group leaders to be ready to add to the discussion with insights from **Why Is This PG-13 Story in the Bible?** (p. 38).

Give each group a "1" card. This can be a "1" cut from construction paper, the number "1" written boldly on an index card, or a playing card bearing the number "1". As the group discusses the questions, have students randomly pass the card to other people. The person holding the card answers the question or makes a comment. If necessary, the leader can redirect the card at times to make sure everyone has an opportunity to speak. If you like, have groups each pick a person to record notes of their discussion.

This story about the power of one certainly has a vengeful twist. Let's get into the heads of the characters and figure out what God was up to.

Team Talk 1: Get into the head of Ehud.

- **What do you think motivates Ehud to take such drastic action?** *(The hard rule of a foreign king. Israel is crying out to God for help. A spiritual leader takes action.)*
- **What example does Ehud give us for making the most of unique characteristics?** *(Being left-handed allowed him to use a surprise motion and catch the king off guard. Whatever special abilities we have, we can use them for the good of others.)*
- **What do you think was going through Ehud's head when he was alone with this powerful and dangerous king?** *(He's looking for an opportunity, reading the situation, perhaps feeling nervous.)*
- **Why do you suppose Ehud acts alone?** *(He answers when God raises him up for the job. Perhaps he doesn't want to expose others to danger. Maybe no one else will help or is as bold as him!)*
- **How would you describe the way Ehud makes decisions?** *(Plans carefully and has a strategy to succeed. But also depends on God to make things happen.)*

Team Talk 2: Get into the heads of Eglon and his servants.

- **Do you think Eglon has any idea it was God who allowed him to have power over Israel? Explain.** *(No, he's a prideful, pagan king. Possibly, but he denied the role of God in his life.)*
- **Why do you think Eglon underestimates the power of one?** *(He assumes he is the only one who matters. He isn't expecting anything from Ehud, one lowly captive.)*
- **The servants are supposed to have Eglon's back. How do they underestimate the power of one?** *(They may have thought one guy couldn't hurt the king. One private meeting couldn't hurt anything.)*

- **How do you think the servants felt when they realized what one Israelite had done?** *(Ashamed of their lack of responsibility. Astounded at Ehud's daring. Afraid of what might come next.)*

Bring your discussion teams back together. Briefly review results of discussions by reviewing written notes or asking for the highlights.

Continue your discussion as a large group by asking questions like:

- **Is the point of this story that God approves of violence? Explain.** *(No, the point is that God raised up someone to deliver his people. It's not the main point, but in the Bible God does sometimes use violence and war to accomplish his will.)*
- **How did God have Ehud's back in this story?** *(He protected him in this daring mission. He gave him the personal strength to accomplish this task.)*
- **Why do you think this story with such violence is in the Bible?** *(This is a good opportunity to remind students of the Key Verse: "He will call upon me, and I will answer him; I will be with him in trouble, I will deliver him and honor him" [Psalm 91:15].)*

Like sheep, God's people tended to wander from him. When that happened, God would get their attention by allowing an enemy king to reign over them for some time. Then God would send a deliverer.

Continue with more large-group discussion:

- **At what points in the story could Ehud have made choices that would have changed what happened?** *(He could have decided not to ask for a personal meeting with the king. He could have backed away from his plan to take the king's life. He could have not called the people to follow him even after his bold actions in the king's palace.)*
- **If we get too fascinated with the violence, what do we miss in this story?** *(How God can use a single person determined to serve him.)*
- **How does this story connect to the kinds of challenges you face? (Allow your students to spend extra time on this question if needed!)**

Ehud's plan put an end to an increasingly dismal reality. Today, God doesn't call his followers to attack greedy rulers, but he knows we have challenges to overcome. Don't underestimate the power of God working through *you*. ✗

Take 3: Critics' Corner (15 to 20 minutes)

Setup: Reinforce the points you want your students to take away from today's lesson.
Props: Group journal with entries from Take 1; **Outtakes** (p. 49); a box of toothpicks
and an empty 20-ounce plastic drink bottle for each relay team; tape or string

QUIET ON THE SET

Grab the group journal and ask students to gather to review the "Success
Story" entries recorded earlier.

ACTION

Consider the POV

Ask students to explore the power of one with these questions:

- **Roxanne and John are stuck until they focus on positive outcomes. Why does
  this approach work?**
- **Are you secure in your "power of one"?** *[Possible answers: a) not really; b)
  sometimes; c) I'm a better team player; d) I usually call it quits before I look
  foolish; e) yes.]*
- **How can students your age build confidence? Is there an approach you're
  most proud of? Tell us about it.**
- **What preparation or training can help keep your power sharp?** *(God's Word
  firmly planted in my heart; compassion; a positive attitude; clubs, jobs, or volunteer and community service where I can use my talents.)*

Draw students' attention to the **POV** on the **Outtakes** page: *Don't underestimate the power of one.* Talk about it for a few minutes; you may even repeat the
POV together.

Understand God's Truth

"If God is for us, who can be against us?" (Romans 8:31) God wants you to call
out to him. But it can't stop there. Be willing to be a part of what you're asking
for. You may be "the power of one"—God's answer in a tough situation.

Ask the group:

- **What have we learned from today's story?** *(God raised up Ehud to deliver his
  people from their cycle of slavery. Ehud responded when God called him.)*

Empowered by God, Ehud got the job done. Why not try something new? Trying your hand at a new skill, club, or volunteer work may uncover a new strength or talent you didn't know you had.

Understand the real message behind this rough-and-tumble Old Testament story. Like Ehud, you too can put yourself in God's hands. And in a difficult, uncertain, or painful situation, God can do something powerful.

Teamwork

"He will call upon me, and I will answer him"—that's the action alert in today's Key Verse. Call on God and he'll answer! Encourage each other to be prepared and ready when your moment comes.

PLAY BACK

Wrap up the meeting with a team-building game that helps students reflect on the power of one. Then close in prayer.

Splinter Group

Needed: a box of toothpicks and an empty plastic drink bottle for each relay team; tape or string
Goal: Collect "points" and win.

How to Play:

Use tape or string to mark start and finish lines (about 20 feet apart) for this relay. At the finish line, line up empty plastic drink bottles (caps off), one for each team. Hand the starting player on each relay team a box of toothpicks.

> For easier play, position bottles on chairs. You also can replace toothpicks with pretzel sticks or dried lentils.

On cue, players will power walk or run to their bottles. Once there, they will open their toothpick boxes and try to drop a single toothpick into the bottle on the floor from a standing position (very challenging!). Players keep at it until they score. (Hint that you might not want to tell them right away: Closing one eye helps.) Players will then close the toothpick boxes and power walk or run back to their team to hand off the box to the next player in line. Play continues until time is called or all players on the team get one toothpick in the bottle.

Teams may need to stop play and collect toothpicks on the floor to finish the relays.

If one team hasn't gotten all members to score a point, the team with the most toothpicks in their bottle wins.

Be sure to encourage students to cheer on their teammates.

One point at a time gains the winning edge. A powerful "one" is a vital link in any strong team. So take aim and deliver!

Close with Prayer

> **Verse-atility:** *When the going gets rough, the tough get God.*

Ask your group to look again at **Outtakes** and repeat today's **Key Verse:** "He will call upon me, and I will answer him; I will be with him in trouble, I will deliver him and honor him" (Psalm 91:15). Then point out this week's *Verse-atility: When the going gets rough, the tough get God.* If time allows, jot the Bible verse in the group journal and have everyone initial it.

Invite students to share prayer requests. Then say: **The "power of one" can be a lonely experience at times. Remember that with prayer you're never alone.**

Allow students to spend time praying silently for each other's requests; this can be a bonding experience for the group. ✘

The Power of One

Characters:
ROXANNE: a middle school girl
JOHN: a middle school guy
Scene: The family room at Roxanne's house
Prop Suggestions: Select any props or costumes you want from the prop box; you may also want to use a TV, remote control, two chairs or comfy bean bag chairs for sitting, and a business class "assignment sheet" . . . or just pretend!

SCRIPT

JOHN:
Are you done with math?

ROXANNE:
Yeah, I finished that. . . . I still need an idea for Business Week for school.

JOHN:
Yeah, me too. *(reading from the school assignment sheet)* **"Assignment: Create a product or service others will want to purchase. Communicate your idea with a written report and oral presentation. Assignments are due Friday."** Friday?!

ROXANNE:
(Takes the sheet and continues to read.) **"This is an independent project. Do your best!"**

JOHN:
Well, we don't have much time.

ROXANNE:
Sophia is making jewelry out of drinking straws and chenille wires. And Ethan? He's putting together a cookbook. Deep-fried Oreos and Twinkies!

JOHN:
Uh-huh. *(Very dry.)* That's hilarious.

(John, fixated on the TV, isn't paying much attention to Roxanne as she speaks.)

ROXANNE:
Sanjay plans to make money as a motivational speaker. . . . He's gonna talk about the time last summer . . . when he saved his little sister from drowning.

JOHN:
Oh yeah—I heard about that. The fire department called him a hero. Wow. I have no clue what I'm going to do.

(Both sit in silence watching TV.)

ROXANNE:
You know, we need to concentrate on what we can do, what we're good at.

JOHN:
Everybody's good at something, right?

ROXANNE:
I like to take pictures of animals. And sunsets.

JOHN:
(Still paying attention only to the TV.) I like watching TV.

ROXANNE:
I like to draw and paint stuff.

(Roxanne has to hit John to get his attention.)

JOHN:
I like to watch TV and play video games.

ROXANNE:
(deep in thought) Maybe I can find a way to put the two together . . .

JOHN:
Watch TV. Play video games. Done. That was easy.

ROXANNE:
C'mon John! We've got to sell this!

JOHN:
(slumping in the chair, pauses) OK, how about this? I like to help the trainers with bandages and wrappings at practice—maybe I could make some money doing that!

ROXANNE:
Sports therapy! It's a service lots of people use . . . and pay for.

JOHN:
I could open up my own practice someday.

ROXANNE:
"Promote overall fitness and health with John Taylor!"

JOHN:
I'm gonna use that, Rox! Hey, I got an idea for you. You can use your photos and art to make greeting cards to sell.

ROXANNE:
Hmmm . . . Three dollars? Three dollars a card sounds right.

JOHN:
We can do this! *(gets up, heading for the door)* Hey, can you stop by practice tomorrow and take pictures of me in action? It'll help with my presentation.

ROXANNE:
(She laughs.) Sure. That'll be ten dollars!

JOHN:
(with a knowing smile) Very funny, Miz Biz!

(John heads for the door.)

(Skit ends; actors join the rest of the group.)

Outtakes

CAST

Ehud: leader of Israel
Eglon: king of Moab
Servants of Eglon: don't have a clue what's happening

MOVIE TRAILER

- Because Israel turned their backs on God, he gave Eglon power over Israel.
- The people cry out to God and he gives them Ehud to save them.
- Ehud goes to see the king with a private message, so Eglon sends the servants out.
- When Ehud is alone with Eglon, he kills him with a sword.
- By the time the servants figure out what happened, Ehud is long gone.
- Ehud leads Israel in attacking and conquering Moab.

Verse-atility: When the going gets rough, the tough get God.

POV: Don't underestimate the power of one.
Key Verse: "He will call upon me, and I will answer him; I will be with him in trouble, I will deliver him and honor him" (Psalm 91:15).

DEADLY FORCE Judges 3:12-30 *(The Message)*
*(We've added a few of our own comments in **bold** below.)*

But the People of Israel went back to doing evil in God's sight. So God made Eglon king of Moab a power against Israel because they did evil in God's sight. He recruited the Ammonites and Amalekites and went out and struck Israel. They took the City of Palms. The People of Israel were in servitude **[slaves]** to Eglon fourteen years.

The People of Israel cried out to God and God raised up for them a savior, Ehud son of Gera, a Benjaminite. He was left-handed. The People of Israel sent tribute **[a hefty tax]** by him to Eglon king of Moab. Ehud made himself a short two-edged sword and strapped it on his right thigh under his clothes. He presented the tribute to Eglon king of Moab. Eglon was grossly fat. After Ehud finished presenting the tribute, he went a little way with the men who had carried it. But when he got as far as the stone images near Gilgal, he went back and said, "I have a private message for you, O King."

The king told his servants, "Leave." They all left.

Ehud approached him—the king was now quite alone in his cool rooftop room—and said, "I have a word of God for you." Eglon stood up from his throne. Ehud reached with his left hand and took his sword from his right thigh and plunged it into the king's big belly. Not only the blade but the hilt went in. The fat closed in over it so he couldn't pull it out. **[Spoiler alert: it's a fatal wound.]** Ehud slipped out by way of the porch and shut and locked the doors of the rooftop room behind him. Then he was gone.

When the servants came, they saw with surprise that the doors to the rooftop room were locked. They said, "He's probably relieving himself in the restroom." **[Nature calls?]**

They waited. And then they worried—no one was coming out of those locked doors. Finally, they got a key and unlocked them. There was their master, fallen on the floor, dead!

While they were standing around wondering what to do, Ehud was long gone. He got past the stone images and escaped to Seirah. When he got there, he sounded the trumpet on Mount Ephraim. **[A very good vibe.]** The People of Israel came down from the hills and joined him. He took his place at their head.

He said, "Follow me, for God has given your enemies—yes, Moab!—to you." They went down after him and secured the fords of the Jordan against the Moabites. They let no one cross over.

At that time, they struck down about ten companies of Moabites, all of them well-fed and robust. Not one escaped. That day Moab was subdued under the hand of Israel.

The land was quiet for eighty years.

4 Deadly Force, the Sequel

Director's Commentary

NOW SHOWING: *Deadly Force, the Sequel*

FROM THE BIBLE: Jael kills an enemy of Israel with a tent stake (Judges 4:1-10, 14-24).

RATED PG-13 FOR: death by tent stake—through the head

POV: Obedience is proof positive that you trust God's plan.

KEY VERSE: "Give me understanding, and I will keep your law and obey it with all my heart" (Psalm 119:34).

The Lesson	Time	What you'll do . . .	How you'll do it . . .	What you'll need . . .
Take 1: Preview	15 to 20 minutes	Start off your lesson by introducing the theme with a relational, creative activity.	Option 1: Kids write IOUs for their parents or guardians and discuss them.	"IOU So Much" handouts (pp. 60, 61), pencils; group journal supplies and marker (*Optional:* chocolate candy pieces)
			Option 2: Students watch a DVD version of "Obedience Rules!" and discuss when it's hard, or easy, to be obedient to the people in their lives. Or, choose to do both.	*Dark and Disturbing Stories from the Bible DVD*, TV and DVD player
Take 2: Feature Presentation	15 to 20 minutes	Dive into the Bible story and explore it together.	Small group and large group discussion	Photocopies of **Outtakes** (p. 62); newsprint or pieces of poster board, markers
Take 3: Critics' Corner	15 to 20 minutes	Help your students grasp God's point of view and wrap things up with a fun team-building activity.	Discussion, game, and prayer	Photocopies of **Outtakes** (p. 62); group journal; pencils, 2 or 3 Nerf-like or foam balls, or newspaper sheets and masking tape

WHY IS THIS PG-13 STORY IN THE BIBLE?

What exactly is Barak's problem? Israel is once again in a cycle where God has allowed a foreign king, Jabin of Hazor, to oppress his people for twenty years. Now God is ready to raise up a new deliverer.

It's supposed to be Barak, according to Deborah, who should be the judge and prophet at this time. God promises victory over Jabin's powerful general, Sisera. Yet Barak hesitates. Is he doubting God's choice? Is he doubting God himself? Because of Barak's response, Deborah says God will use a woman to get the job done—and that's a big slap in the face to a man in Barak's time and culture.

Deborah puts on her military hat and mobilizes Barak and ten thousand other men. They face off in battle against the great Sisera's army and his nine hundred iron chariots—and it's a complete rout. Despite having the advantage of chariots, Sisera is left with no option but to flee on foot and look for some place to hide.

And now for the real hero of the story: Jael. Her husband is on friendly terms with Jabin, but Jael remembers that her people (the Kenites) go back a long way with the Israelites. Their ancestor was the brother-in-law of Moses, Israel's great leader generations earlier. So, despite what her husband may think, Jael throws her lot in with Israel, lures Sisera into a trap by inviting him into her tent, covers him up while the exhausted general sleeps—and then kills him by driving a tent stake through his head.

To someone of her time, Jael's actions would have been considered horrendous—but not just because of a gruesome murder that we modern readers react to. Rather, the big "crime" here is that Jael violates hospitality customs, which required her to protect her guest from any harm (not inflict it!). On top of that, her family was formally at peace with Jabin and she contradicted her husband's decision.

Jael is a nobody—a woman, a nomad. Barak is a military commander chosen by God for certain victory. But because Barak hesitates, God uses Jael to get the job done. Her loyalties and quick thinking in unsettled times powerfully illustrate how God often uses unlikely people to advance his plans.

Connecting with Community

Log on to www.darkanddisturbing.com to connect with other ministries:

- Check out a sample video of other students in action.
- Share with other leaders at the PG-13 forum about what's working in your ministry, what's not, or how you used Dark and Disturbing or Shocking and Scandalous this week.
- Or ask for input about other aspects of middle school ministry.

This Bible story will help middle schoolers see that when God has a plan, he carries through. It's up to us whether we'll be a part of his plan or not.

Take It to Your Students

Here are some key points for your students with this lesson:

- God has a plan. Be willing to be part of it.
- God doesn't force anyone to obey him.
- Obedience shows trust in God's direction. ✗

Deadly Force, the Sequel: The Lesson

Take 1: Preview (15 to 20 minutes)

Setup: This activity will set up the day's Bible story in a relational way as students write IOUs that honor their parents or guardians.

Props: "IOU So Much" handouts (pp. 60, 61), one per student, pencils; supplies for the journal option you've chosen, marker (*Optional:* a bag of chocolate candy pieces) Or play the corresponding clip on the *Dark and Disturbing Stories from the Bible DVD*—or do both activities.

QUIET ON THE SET

To launch the lesson:

- Welcome everyone to the group. Use first names or preferred nicknames and introduce visitors. After your students have had some time to socialize, pull them in and have them get comfortable.
- Go over your Rules of Engagement if needed. (See the Rules of Engagement suggestions on p. 6 for more information.)
- Review the journaling method you've chosen for your group. (See Create a Group Journal on p. 10 for more information.)

ACTION

Pass out pencils and "IOU So Much" handouts, one per person, and lead the group in completing the top part of the page.

Parents spend a lot of time thinking about you and what's best for you. Even though you may not feel like it sometimes, they really care. Your obedience and respect are a good way to show that you care too. Fill in the top portion of your handout with words or phrases that honor your parents or guardians. Then circle the key words. We'll do the word search in just a bit.

Nothing says "dull and boring" to middle schoolers like the silent roar of white noise during what's meant to be a fun activity. So set an upbeat tone by playing teen-friendly music in the background as students fill out their "IOU So Much" handouts.

PLAY BACK

Have everybody gather together and lead students in reviewing their "IOU So Much" entries by giving the following instructions (allow time for students to respond to each prompt):

> If you wrote the word _love_ on your handout, stand.
> If you wrote something about food, sit.
> If you wrote words like _obedience, thanks, respect, gratitude,_ or _honor,_ stand.
> If you wrote a specific action or activity, sit.
> If you wrote _money,_ stand.
> If you wrote _hugs_ or _kisses,_ sit.

If you've got the chocolate candy pieces, pass them out and ask volunteers to share some of the remaining entries from their sheets while enjoying their treats. Spend time reflecting on the similarities and differences between what students wrote. Write "IOU So Much" in the group journal, record today's date, and jot down students' overall impressions.

Prompt everybody to complete the rest of their "IOU So Much" handouts. Have students use their circled IOU words to create an original word search puzzle. Explain that words can go vertically, horizontally, or diagonally. They should then fill in all the remaining spaces with random letters. If time permits, have students trade papers and try to solve each other's puzzles. Afterward, make sure everyone gets their paper back.

Another option, if you prefer, is to suggest that students ask their siblings or parents to complete the puzzles at home.

Take your IOU handouts home and share them with your parents. They'll be fired up that you did!

Parents have an important job: setting the rules. They try to set rules that are consistent and that show a mutual respect for all family members.

DVD Option: Play the "Obedience Rules!" video on the *Dark and Disturbing Stories from the Bible DVD* to kick-start your group's discussion of the next few questions, or do the activity and play the video. After the video, ask your students:
• Who's the main rule-maker in your home?
• When you were a little kid, what's one rule you had a hard time obeying? Explain.
• What's one rule in your life—at home or at school—that you wish you could change? How would you change it?
• In your home, can you choose whether or not to obey the rules? Explain.
• Is it hard or easy for you to be obedient to the people in authority in your life? Why?
• Is it hard or easy for you to be obedient to God? Why?

Obedience gets the hamster fed, the garbage taken out, the play performed, the conference finals won. To obey—even when you'd rather not—shows maturity.

With weakness in the ranks, two women step up to obey God by doing an officer's job in today's Old Testament brawl. It's a cast of thousands, a mediocre commander, and a piercing weapon of doom in *Deadly Force, the Sequel,* up next. ✘

Take 2: Feature Presentation   (15 to 20 minutes)

Setup: Your students will take a close look at the story of Deborah, Barak, and Jael and discuss the connection between obedience and trust.

Props: Photocopies of **Outtakes** (p. 62); newsprint sheets or pieces of poster board, markers

Optional: Bibles

QUIET ON THE SET

Pass out copies of **Outtakes**, one per student.
Optional: Have students grab their own Bibles.

ACTION

Use **Outtakes** to introduce and teach the Bible story. First, briefly introduce the **Cast** and make sure your students know who's who. Next, use **Movie Trailer** to cover the highlights of the Bible background and story. Then read the Bible story (Judges 4:1-10, 14-24) out loud from **Outtakes** or have a volunteer read it. If you prefer, ask students to read the entire passage (4:1-24) aloud from their Bibles.

PLAY BACK

Divide your group into two or more small teams for discussion with an older teen or adult leader for each group. If possible, plan to make the groups all guys or all girls. Girls will explore the motivations of Deborah and Jael (Girl Talk, below) while the guys get into the heads of Barak and Sisera (Guy Talk). Remind leaders to enhance discussion with insights from **Why Is This PG-13 Story in the Bible?** (p. 51).

Give each discussion team two sheets of newsprint (or poster board) and markers. Have the girls draw likenesses of Deborah and Jael and have the guys draw Barak and Sisera. As students discuss the questions, have team members doodle speech balloons for each character and write their thoughts inside.

Similarities exist between our lead characters. Let's uncover what they are.

Girl Talk: Get into the heads of Deborah and Jael.

• **Deborah and Jael don't have much in common in their lives, but in what ways do they think alike?** *(Do the right thing; make decisions; be bold for God; stick to God's way.)*

• **How does Deborah show her inner strength?** *(Called for Barak; led the military attack.)*

• **How about Jael?** *(She thought for herself instead of just doing what her husband had decided. She broke the "rules" in order to help Israel.)*

• **What do you think were the motivations behind what Deborah and Jael did?** *(Deborah was following God's directions. Jael was honoring old loyalties.)*

• **As a girl, how are these two women examples for you?**

Guy Talk: Get into the heads of Barak and Sisera.

• **Barak and Sisera were both military commanders. What else did they have in common?** *(They both showed moments of cowardice in this story. Both sought the help of women.)*

• **Why do you think Barak hesitated to act? What would you think, feel, or do in his shoes?**

Just a reminder that we've included examples of possible student answers to some of the discussion questions in these lessons. You'll see them in *italics*. If your students get stuck on a question, share one of the sample answers to help them get their discussion started.

- **Who did Barak trust? Who did Sisera trust?** *(Barak trusted Deborah's human presence more than he trusted God's directions. Sisera trusted himself; Sisera also trusted Jael.)*
- **Name some words that describe what Barak was made of on the inside. How about Sisera?**
- **As a guy, would you want to be like either of these men? Explain.**

Bring the discussion teams back together. Briefly review what they talked about by reading out loud the speech balloons for each character.

Continue your discussion as a large group by asking questions like:

- **How does God show us in this story that he has a plan we can trust?**
- **Who do you think is the real hero of this story? Why?**
- **Why do you think this story is in the Bible?** *(This is a good opportunity to remind students of the Key Verse: "Give me understanding, and I will keep your law and obey it with all my heart" [Psalm 119:34].)*

God's plans have a very, very long life. Today's characters must decide if they're in it for the long haul.

Use these key questions to prompt more large-group discussion:

- **This story is full of choices. Name some that could have changed the story.**
- **What does obedience have to do with trust in this story?**
- **What does obedience have to do with trust in your life?**

Deborah and Jael were women to be reckoned with. Their bravery, tenacious spirit, and obedience spoke louder than words ever could. When the dust settled on the battlefield that day, obedience had conquered and God's will prevailed. ✘

Take 3: Critics' Corner   (15 to 20 minutes)

Setup: Reinforce the points you want your students to take away from today's lesson.

Props: Group journal with entries from Take 1, pencils; **Outtakes** (p. 62); 2 or 3 Nerf-like or foam balls, or newspaper sheets and masking tape

QUIET ON THE SET

Grab the group journal and review students' impressions from Take 1.

ACTION

Consider the POV

Discuss the idea that trust leads to obedience.

When you were little, you obeyed because others told you it was the right thing to do. You trusted their guidance. Now that you're older, you make more decisions for yourself. Ultimately, you can choose to obey God because he's given you his Word that he's trustworthy.

Ask the group:

- What do you understand now about God's presence in your life that you didn't understand when you were younger? Give some examples.
- Do you trust that God has a plan with your name on it? Why or why not?
- What difference would a personalized plan make in your life?
- Name some ways you trust God. What do you trust him to be? What do you trust him to do?
- What are your go-to Bible verses (or Bible stories) that help strengthen your trust in God's plan? *(You might want to have students look up and read aloud passages like Jeremiah 29:11, Psalm 56:4, Proverbs 3:5, 6, and John 14:1.)*

Encourage students to jot their favorite trust verses in the group journal. Then draw students' attention to **Outtakes** again and ask them to repeat today's **POV:** *Obedience is proof positive that you trust God's plan.*

Understand God's Truth

God says what he means and means what he says. But he won't *force* anyone to obey him. Rather, he chooses to work through you with your permission. Deborah and Jael's obedience was proof positive that they trusted God's plan.

Ask the group:

- **What have we learned from today's story?** *(When God has a plan, he carries it through; others can choose whether to be part of the plan or not.)*

- **What was Barak's obedience challenge?** *(Dual interests—allegiance to God and what's-in-it-for-me?—weakened Barak's leadership, making him a sidekick to the powerful prophetess Deborah.)*

The Canaanite general fled to Heber's camp where Jael warmly welcomed him and then did him in. Cold! Yet, Jael's quick-thinking and, yes, brutal act in wartime eased the suffering of thousands of God's children.

Teamwork

We're a team genuinely interested in sharing God's vision with the world. We do the will of God from the heart, knowing that obedience puts us in touch with his Spirit. When called upon to act, we'll answer obediently.

PLAY BACK

Wrap up the meeting with a fun team-building game that helps students reflect on the self-discipline of obedience. Then close in prayer.

Simon Says

For large groups of twenty or more, use three balls.

Needed: 2 or 3 Nerf-like or foam balls, or newspaper sheets and masking tape
Goal: Throw and catch the balls when "Simon Says."

How to Play:

Use two Nerf-like or foam balls or make your own soft balls using newspaper sheets and masking tape. To make a soft ball, loosely crumple a newspaper sheet to the size of a large orange. Tape around and around the paper until none of the newspaper can be seen. Keep the ball soft and mushy.

Ask your group to spread out. Say: **When I say "Simon says throw," throw the balls around the room to each other.**

Balls should be thrown quickly from player to player but still be catchable. Players must keep an eye out for balls coming from two or three directions! Catchers that drop catchable balls sit out play.

After letting it go on for a bit, say: **Simon says stop!**

Play stops. Play resumes when you repeat: **Simon says throw!**

At your choosing, say: **Stop!**

Those who stop throwing or catching sit out play (Simon didn't say!). Mix it up as you would any Simon Says game. Appoint a referee who can keep an eye on play to declare players in or out. Play continues until only one player remains standing.

After the game, say: **Obeying God is a spiritual discipline. But think of it as an opportunity too. More important than ever, it will help you lead in real-life situations.**

Option: Replace "Simon says throw" with other actions such as "throw underhand," "throw under your leg," "throw with your left hand," and so on. Don't forget "Simon says"!

Verse-atility: *Lord, help me know the real you and I will obey.*

Close with Prayer

Ask your group to look again at **Outtakes** and repeat today's **Key Verse:** "Give me understanding, and I will keep your law and obey it with all my heart" (Psalm 119:34). Then point out this week's *Verse-atility: Lord, help me know the real you and I will obey.* If time permits, jot the verse in the group journal and have everyone initial it.

Invite students to share prayer requests, especially those that connect with the main idea of the lesson. Pray together for students' requests, then prompt everyone to pray silently about areas in their lives in which they need God's help to be more obedient. ✘

IOU So Much

PART 1 DIRECTIONS:

Here's your chance to compose original IOUs for Mom and/or Dad or a guardian. Why? Because they're worth it! Some examples include: a poem, a card, a favorite snack or lunch, breakfast in bed, a simple thank you, a back rub, lots of love, and so on. When you're done, circle 8 to 10 key words in the phrases you've written.

Dear (fill in the blank)_____.

#1 IOU _a (smile) and "have a nice day!"_____

#2 IOU _____

#3 IOU _____

#4 IOU _____

#5 IOU _____

#6 IOU _____

#7 IOU _____

#8 IOU _____

#9 IOU _____

#10 IOU _____

PART 2 DIRECTIONS:

Use your circled IOU words to create a word search puzzle. Words can go vertically, horizontally, or diagonally. Fill in extra spaces with random letters.

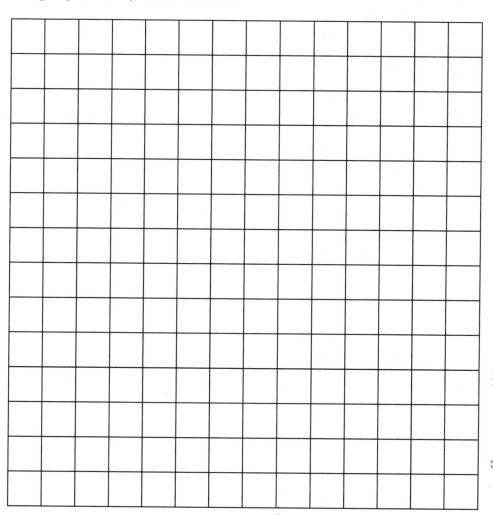

Outttakes

CAST

Deborah: a judge and prophet leading Israel
Barak: a military leader of Israel who's afraid of Sisera
Sisera: commander of the army of Canaan under King Jabin
Jael: wife of Heber; Heber is friendly with Jabin but Jael defects to help Israel

MOVIE TRAILER

- Because Israel kept on doing evil, God let Jabin, king of Canaan, rule over Israel.
- Deborah brings a message from God that it's time to attack Sisera, the commander of Jabin's army; Barak is to lead Israel.
- Barak is afraid of Sisera and wants Deborah to go with him.
- Deborah and Barak lead Israel's army. They wipe out Sisera's army, but Sisera escapes.
- Jael invites Sisera into her tent. He thinks she will protect him, but instead she kills him—with a tent stake driven through the head.
- Barak comes looking for Sisera and Jael shows Barak that Sisera is dead.

Verse-atility: Lord, help me know the real you and I will obey.

POV: Obedience is proof positive that you trust God's plan.
Key Verse: "Give me understanding, and I will keep your law and obey it with all my heart" (Psalm 119:34).

DEADLY FORCE, THE SEQUEL Judges 4:1-10, 14-24 (The Message) (We've added a few of our own comments in **bold** below.)

The People of Israel kept right on doing evil in God's sight. With Ehud dead, God sold them off to Jabin king of Canaan who ruled from Hazor. **[Do the crime, do the time.]** Sisera, who lived in Harosheth Haggoyim, was the commander of his army. The People of Israel cried out to God because he had cruelly oppressed them with his nine hundred iron chariots for twenty years.

Deborah was a prophet, the wife of Lappidoth. She was judge over Israel at that time. She held court under Deborah's Palm between Ramah and Bethel in the hills of Ephraim. The People of Israel went to her in matters of justice.

She sent for Barak son of Abinoam from Kedesh in Naphtali and said to him, "It has become clear that God, the God of Israel, commands you: Go to Mount Tabor and prepare for battle. Take ten companies of soldiers from Naphtali and Zebulun. I'll take care of getting Sisera, the leader of Jabin's army, to the Kishon River with all his chariots and troops. And I'll make sure you win the battle."

Barak said, "If you go with me, I'll go. But if you don't go with me, I won't go." **[Riiiight . . .]**

She said, "Of course I'll go with you. But understand that with a **[busted]** attitude like that, there'll be no glory in it for you. God will use a woman's hand to take care of Sisera."

Deborah got ready and went with Barak to Kedesh.

. . . Deborah said to Barak, "Charge! This very day God has given you victory over Sisera. Isn't God marching before you?"

Barak charged down the slopes of Mount Tabor, his ten companies following him.

God routed Sisera—all those **[900 horsepower!]** chariots, all those troops!—before Barak. Sisera jumped out of his chariot and ran. Barak chased the chariots and troops all the way to Harosheth Haggoyim. Sisera's entire fighting force was killed—not one man was left.

Meanwhile Sisera, running for his life, headed for the tent of Jael, wife of Heber the Kenite. Jabin king of Hazor and Heber the Kenite were on good terms with one another. Jael stepped out to meet Sisera and said, "Come in, sir. Stay here with me. Don't be afraid." **[A perilous welcome . . .]**

So he went with her into her tent. She covered him with a blanket.

He said to her, "Please, a little water. I'm thirsty."

She opened a bottle of milk, gave him a drink, and then covered him up again.

He then said, "Stand at the tent flap. If anyone comes by and asks you, 'Is there anyone here?' tell him, 'No, not a soul.'"

Then while he was fast asleep from exhaustion, Jael wife of Heber took a tent peg and hammer, tiptoed toward him, and drove the tent peg through his temple and all the way into the ground. He convulsed and died. **[Violence hazard!]**

Barak arrived in pursuit of Sisera. Jael went out to greet him. She said, "Come, I'll show you the man you're looking for." He went with her and there he was—Sisera, stretched out, dead, with a tent peg through his temple.

On that day God subdued Jabin king of Canaan before the People of Israel. The People of Israel pressed harder and harder on Jabin king of Canaan until there was nothing left of him.

Director's Commentary

NOW SHOWING: *Who Wants to Be Famous?*

FROM THE BIBLE: Solomon's greatness spirals down (1 Kings 10:23-25, 11:1-13).

RATED PG-13 FOR: sexual obsession

POV: Recognize your weaknesses; stick with self-control.

KEY VERSE: "What good is it for a man to gain the whole world, and yet lose or forfeit his very self?" (Luke 9:25).

The Lesson	Time	What you'll do . . .	How you'll do it . . .	What you'll need . . .
Take 1: Preview	15 to 20 minutes	Start off your lesson by introducing the theme with a relational, creative activity.	Option 1: Students act out "And the Winner Is . . ." drama and discuss it.	5 photocopies of "And the Winner Is . . ." script (pp.73, 74); markers, group journal supplies (*Optional:* items from your prop box, including books and notebooks for your actors; movie snacks for your audience)
			Option 2: Students watch a DVD version of "And the Winner Is . . ." and discuss it. Or, choose to do both.	*Dark and Disturbing Stories from the Bible DVD*, TV and DVD player; markers, group journal supplies
Take 2: Feature Presentation	15 to 20 minutes	Dive into the Bible story and explore it together.	Small group and large group discussion	Photocopies of **Outtakes** (p. 75), a dictionary for each group *Optional:* Bibles
Take 3: Critics' Corner	15 to 20 minutes	Help your students grasp God's point of view and wrap things up with a fun team-building activity.	Discussion, game, and prayer	**Outtakes** (p. 75); group journal; letter-size paper, pens or pencils

WHY IS THIS PG-13 STORY IN THE BIBLE?

Solomon, a son of David by his wife Bathsheba, strategized his way through fractious family relationships to be his father's choice for king. His reign lasted forty years, the same length as David's. However, their kingships were vastly different. David's mission was to acquire and establish the land; he was a warrior. Solomon's job was to build a nation and secure its future.

Famous around the world for his wisdom, Solomon established administrative districts for efficient government and pursued widespread international relations to benefit Israel. His territory included trade routes linking Africa, Asia Minor, Arabia, and Asia. The commerce through these zones generated impressive income. People came from far and wide to hear Solomon's wisdom and offer a steady stream of gifts. Extensive building programs provided the infrastructure of Israel—cities specifically designed to store provisions of food and armaments, as well as fortifications around key locations such as Jerusalem. Solomon also constructed an elaborate palace for himself and a lavish permanent temple for the nation's worship. In many ways, Solomon's reign was the high point of Israel's history up to this time.

However, this was no fairy-tale kingdom. Solomon's building programs were expensive and difficult. They consumed economic resources in the form of absurdly high taxation, and the workforce came through conscripting laborers against their will. Even more significant, though, was the effect that Solomon's cosmopolitan policies had on him personally.

Solomon loved women. Hundreds of them. In fact, he married seven hundred women, and he had another three hundred concubines, a subordinate level of wife. Many of these relationships were political in origin, of course, but Solomon was vulnerable when it came to the wishes of his wives. They brought their foreign gods and religious practices to Solomon's kingdom, and he allowed it. Shamelessly and without remorse, he built altars to foreign gods.

By marrying foreign women and then allowing their religious activities, Solomon violated two clear and emphatic dimensions of God's law. This caused God to be angry with him and to promise to tear the kingdom away. Solomon began to struggle to maintain control. When he died, latent unrest ripped the nation in two, and it was never again united.

This story will remind middle schoolers how easy it is to be enticed by things we know in our hearts are wrong.

Take It to Your Students

Here are some key points for your students in this lesson:

- You have control over your choices.
- If getting what you want means taking advantage of others, what you want is wrong.
- If you think you're weakness-free, think again.

Who Wants to Be Famous?: The Lesson

Take 1: Preview (15 to 20 minutes)

Setup: This activity will set up the day's Bible story in a relational way as students perform the "And the Winner Is . . . " script and imagine a celebrity life.

Set design: Create a relaxed atmosphere for *Preview.* Ask students to sit on the floor in a circle on pillows, seat cushions, or colorful mats. The drama will be performed in the middle. Popcorn or movie snacks will help set a movie mood.

Makeup and effects: For today's drama, consider having students rummage through your one-size-fits-all prop box.

Props: Supplies for the journal option you've chosen, markers; 5 copies of the "And the Winner Is . . ." skit (pp. 73, 74); or the *Dark and Disturbing Stories from the Bible DVD* with TV and DVD player; or both

(*Optional:* movie snacks for your audience)

QUIET ON THE SET

To launch the lesson:

- Welcome everyone to the group. Use first names or preferred nicknames and introduce visitors. After your students have had some time to socialize, pull them in and have them get comfortable.

- Go over your Rules of Engagement, if needed. (See the Rules of Engagement suggestions on p. 6 for more information.)
- Review the journaling component you've chosen for your group. (See Create a Group Journal on p. 10 for more information.)

ACTION

Option: If you want, make a video of your students' live performance. Play it back for the group, the group and parents, or maybe the entire church.

Either have students perform the "And the Winner Is . . ." skit, watch "And the Winner Is . . ." on the *Dark and Disturbing Stories from the Bible DVD*, or do both. If you choose to have students perform the skit live, give copies of the script to the actors and have them prep by reading through their parts a time or two. Also invite the actors to rummage through the prop box for items to enhance their performance. (Since the scene is a school library, books and notebooks would be appropriate.)

PLAY BACK

Option: If you want, use a pop culture example to set the scene for the skit by having your group watch a few minutes of a reality talent television show that features teenagers and young adults.

Spend time reflecting on "And the Winner Is . . ." with your group. Don't edit your students' responses; allow them to discuss freely. Have a volunteer write "And the Winner Is . . ." and today's date in the group journal, then record the group's impression.

Give every student the opportunity to comment or to journal, even if it's just to initial in agreement with posted entries.

Use the questions below to get a group discussion going after the skit, DVD clip, or both.

It's the answer to every heart's desire, right? *Fame!*

- Which is your favorite reality talent show?
- Do you think sudden fame or popularity changes the show's winners? Explain.
- If you could be a star at anything, what would it be?
- With fame, what would you never have to do again?
- What would you have to start doing?
- If you could be world famous—with all the benefits and all the problems that come with fame—would you want to be? Why or why not?

Today's must-watch star is one of the wisest men who ever lived. He is world renowned, the best of the best, a true hall-of-famer. But with noble stature comes a flock of wives and lovers—one thousand to be Bible-exact. Self-control is clearly MIA (missing in action) for this flawed celeb in *Who Wants to Be Famous?*, up next. ✗

Take 2: Feature Presentation   (15 to 20 minutes)

Setup: Your students will take a close look at the story of Solomon and discuss the dangers of losing self-control.

Props: Photocopies of **Outtakes** (p. 75); several dictionaries, paper, and pens
   Optional: Bibles

QUIET ON THE SET

Pass out copies of **Outtakes**, one per student. Optional: Have students grab their own Bibles.

ACTION

Use **Outtakes** to introduce and teach the Bible story. First, briefly introduce the **Cast** and make sure your students know who's who. Next, use **Movie Trailer** to cover the highlights of the Bible background and story. Then read the Bible story (1 Kings 10:23-25; 11:1-13) out loud from **Outtakes** or have a volunteer read it. If you prefer, ask students to read the passages aloud from their Bibles.

PLAY BACK

Divide your group into two or more small teams for discussion with an adult or older team leader for each group. If possible, plan to make the groups all guys or all girls. Girls will explore the perspectives of the one thousand women in the story (Girl Talk, below), while the guys will look at Solomon's motivations and choices (Guy Talk). If your group is small, you can discuss all the questions together, but choose discussion questions with sensitivity. Remind group leaders to be ready to enhance discussion with insights from **Why Is This PG-13 Story in the Bible?** (p. 64).

   Give each group a dictionary, paper, and pens. Have students look up the key words featured for each group in their discussion questions, then relate the

Just a reminder that we've got some helpful insights about forming small groups in the Team Talk Small Groups section on pp. 10, 11.

definitions they find to the story characters. Ask someone in each small group to read the definitions out loud, and someone else to jot notes on the discussion.

King Solomon Live! Solomon very well could have been a finalist in a "Top Celeb of All Time" reality show. But as we now know, the top judge votes him off. Let's go backstage and see why.

Girl Talk: Get into the heads of the one thousand women.

- Look up the word *beguile*. How do females sometimes beguile to get what they want from guys? (If you're in an all-girls group, have an honest discussion about the games girls sometimes play and who gets hurt.)

- Look up the word *seduce*. How did the women in the story persuade Solomon to do wrong through their seduction? (*They persuaded him to leave his God and to follow their false gods.*)

- Solomon's wives took advantage of his weakness to get what they wanted. Is that ever OK? Explain. (*Taking advantage of another's weakness does not demonstrate God's unselfish love.*)

- Do you think Solomon's wives had any responsibility for his downfall? Why or why not? (Note: this could be argued either way. Women in biblical times did not have the freedom to choose who to marry as women do today. But even though their marriages were often political alliances, Solomon's wives likely understood their power to influence him. In the end, though, Solomon was responsible for his own choices.)

Guy Talk: Get into the head of Solomon.

- Solomon was obsessed with women. Why did this become a huge weakness in his life? (*They turned him away from God to their own beliefs. He lost perspective on what is right.*)

- Look up the word *defy*. How does the definition relate to what Solomon did in his relationship with God? (*He defied the things God and his earthly father, David, had clearly taught him.*)

- Look up the word *abandon*. Is it possible to partially abandon God? Why or why not? (*This can make for some great discussion!*)

- **Solomon let his popularity and wisdom go to his head. Why does power so easily lead a person to lose self-control?** *(You begin to think you are above the standards everyone else must follow. You think you are not accountable to anyone.)*

Bring the discussion teams back together. Briefly review the results of the team discussions by talking about the definitions students found and the major issues they talked about.

Continue your discussion as a large group by asking questions like:

- **Where does Solomon go wrong? Where could he have chosen differently?**
- **Do you think the one thousand women have any responsibility?** *(Yes—they knowingly lured him away from God. No—Solomon is responsible for his own choices.)*
- **Why do you think this story is in the Bible?** *(This is a good opportunity to remind students of the Key Verse: "What good is it for a man to gain the whole world, and yet lose or forfeit his very self?" [Luke 9:25].)*

Solomon was famously and wildly popular—beyond even today's celebrity standards. And smart? Like nobody you'll ever meet. But when a person considers it his absolute right to do whatever his heart desires, downfall is inevitable.

Continue on with more large-group discussion:

- **Review the end of the story on Outtakes. What was the result of Solomon's loss of self-control?** *(God said he would take the kingdom away from his family line.)*
- **What would it have taken for Solomon to turn things around?** *(Recognize his weakness. Turn back to God.)*
- **What does this story have to do with your life?**

Once upon a time Solomon wanted to please God. But that was back in the day. A fatal flaw makes him vulnerable and eventually guarantees his bad choices. **✗**

Take 3: Critics' Corner (15 to 20 minutes)

Setup: Reinforce the points you want your students to take away from today's lesson.
Props: Group journal with entries from Take 1; **Outtakes** (p. 75); letter-size paper, pens or pencils

QUIET ON THE SET

Grab the group journal and review together the "And the Winner Is . . . " entries recorded during Take 1.

ACTION

Consider the POV

Discuss the idea that celebrity culture is all about fame. Say: **As we've discussed, popularity and fame are not a free pass from self-control.**

Use the group journal and make a list together of situations in which middle schoolers have a fair degree of control (food choices, clothes, hairstyles, clubs to join, friendships). Follow up with a separate list of "little-or-no-control" situations (going to school or possibly church, homework, chores, curfew, sickness, divorce on the part of others they know, death).

Ask the group:

• **How does self-control help you manage the emotional ups and downs in life? Share a real-life example from your own experience.** *(Don't be quick to satisfy every need; practice patience; cool down to relax and regroup; think before speaking or reacting; consider outcomes; understand God's way to help; learn from life's experiences and do better next time.)*

Draw students' attention to the **POV** on the **Outtakes** handout: *Recognize your weaknesses; stick with self-control.*

Understand God's Truth

King Solomon wrote the Song of Songs, Ecclesiastes, and the Book of Proverbs, all found in your Bible. These books are a testament to his wisdom. But even a star king is not an exception to God's rule. He was as accountable for his behavior as I am for mine and you are for yours.

Ask the group:

• **What have we learned from today's story?** *(King Solomon broke faith with God by refusing to give up his obsession with women.)*

• **Celebrity sighting! I love God, but I still want to be famous. Is that wrong?** *(No, but remember today's Key Verse: "What good is it for a man to gain the whole world, and yet lose or forfeit his very self?" [Luke 9:25].)*

A "weakness protection program" would have come in handy for King Solomon, don't you think? Examine your behavior this week. Spot the things that cause you to stumble again and again. Once you do, you'll be better equipped to get a handle on them.

Teamwork

We all have weaknesses—but we don't have to let them trip us up. When we feel tempted or when our self-control is wavering, we can turn to each other for backup. We can trust one another for accountability and encouragement.

PLAY BACK

Wrap up the meeting with a team-building game that helps students reflect on the connection between self-control and achieving their dreams. Then close in prayer.

Dream Search

Needed: letter-size paper, pens or pencils
Goal: Match skills to the right person.

> For this activity, make sure students don't write their names on their papers!

How to Play:

Hand each student a piece of paper. Have players write today's **Key Verse** at the top of the page: "What good is it for a man to gain the whole world, and yet lose or forfeit his very self?" (Luke 9:25).

Ask the group: **How would you describe your "self" to someone who didn't know you?**

Have students write on their papers one thing about themselves they're especially proud of—a skill, talent, or ability. *Important: caution your students against writing anything too private, because others will see the papers if you play this game as written here.*

Now, jot down a dream you hope to fulfill someday. Perhaps it's hiking the tallest peaks in the world, becoming a missionary, playing in the NFL, becoming a Tony-winning Broadway star, or serving God as a medical professional. *Don't* **write your names on your papers.**

Give students a minute to jot down their dreams.

Have your group form two lines that are basically equal in length, about ten feet apart and facing each other. Ask students to crumple up their papers. Then shout: **Snowball fight!** After a minute or so of throwing the paper

The Verse-ality option is a middle school-friendly, personalized rewording of the Key Verse. Use it to help your students really get what the Key Verse is all about.

Verse-ality: *Who I am has little to do with fame and fortune.*

Option: Middle schoolers need a prayer that is comforting, reinforces their beliefs, and is immediate and well-known in times of weakness. If you want, wrap up this lesson by having the group find the Lord's Prayer in their Bibles (Matthew 6:9-13) and recite it together. Or if you'd like, lead them through *The Message* paraphrase of the passage:
Our Father in heaven,
Reveal who you are.
Set the world right;
Do what's best—as above, so below.
Keep us alive with three square meals.
Keep us forgiven with you and forgiving others.
Keep us safe from ourselves and the Devil.
You're in charge!
You can do anything you want!
You're ablaze in beauty!
Yes. Yes. Yes.

wads back and forth, halt the blizzard! Have students reach down and pick up the "snowball" nearest them and try to match the words to the person who wrote them. After everybody's found their snowball's "owner," with class permission and mutual respect, prompt students to read some of the entries out loud.

After the game, say: **As any star performer knows, it takes practice to be exceptional. Self-control is a necessary life skill. Practice it like you would any other ability. It will heighten self-awareness and lead to self-discovery. Both will help you follow your dreams in a way that honors God and yourself.**

Close with Prayer

Ask your group to look again at **Outtakes** and repeat today's **Key Verse:** "What good is it for a man to gain the whole world, and yet lose or forfeit his very self?" (Luke 9:25). Then point out this week's *Verse-ality: Who I am has little to do with fame and fortune.* If time allows, jot the verse in the group journal and have everyone initial it.

Invite students to share prayer requests, especially those that relate to following their dreams or to struggles with self-control. Pray that God will help your students manage their stress levels rather than let them lead to a loss of self-control. Also pray that God will help them stay in control of the strong emotions they will experience. ✘

And the Winner Is . . .

Characters:
DAVID and JAKE: two middle school guys
ASHLEY and MAKAYLA: two middle school girls
Scene: School library. Students are hanging out, taking a break from studying.
Prop Suggestions: Select any props or costumes you want from the prop box; these might include books and notebooks for the students.

SCRIPT

ASHLEY *(to MAKAYLA)*:
Have you seen the show "Who Wants to Be the Next Top Performer?"

MAKAYLA:
Oh my gosh, yes. I love that show.

ASHLEY:
Me too.

DAVID *(entering and speaking to JAKE)*:
Hey, why aren't you at basketball practice?

JAKE:
Oh, those are the younger guys. I play later.

MAKAYLA:
Did you hear about Emma?

ASHLEY:
She's going to be on the show "Who Wants to Be the Next Top Performer?" She's going to New York City this weekend.

DAVID:
Whoa! *(He obviously had not heard this news.)*

MAKAYLA:
She can sing *and* dance. I'm so jealous.

DAVID:
She was really good in that talent show last spring.

JAKE:
Emma rocked. It's hard to believe she's from our little town!

MAKAYLA:
Her whole family is flying with her. I wish I could go . . .

DAVID:
We can say we knew her when . . .

JAKE:
I'll bet she'll need an agent.

ASHLEY:
(thoughtfully) **Do you think Emma will still be Emma . . . even if she wins?**

DAVID:
Sure. Why wouldn't she be? But hey—nothing wrong with quittin' school and being famous!

JAKE:
(shaking his head) **She won't do that.**

DAVID:
Well, with fame comes cash, a new house, new car . . .

MAKAYLA:
You're crazy. Emma doesn't even have her license.

DAVID:
(excitedly) **I know what I'd do . . . I'd get the latest in anything digital.**

ASHLEY:
I'd get new hair, new clothes, new accessories. I'd be the new me!

MAKAYLA:
(nodding in agreement) **Wouldn't that make everything easier? . . .**

JAKE:
Get. Get. Get. You guys sound like get-aholics.

MAKAYLA:
(playfully sarcastic) **Oh no! Stop me before I spend again!** *(The others laugh.)*

JAKE:
Well, the money's great. But guys, Ashley's right. Sometimes success can change people.

DAVID:
That's what success is for! Dude, you make it sound like a bad thing.

ASHLEY:
We're just saying that when people win big, sometimes they lose something too.

DAVID:
That won't be Emma. She'll do it up right.

ASHLEY:
I hope so . . .

JAKE:
Well . . . she's gotta win first!

(Skit ends; actors return to group.)

Outtakes

CAST

Solomon: king of Israel
1,000 women: wives and mistresses of Solomon
Rezon: king of Aram
Rehoboam: a rebel against Solomon

MOVIE TRAILER

- King Solomon is world famous for being wise and rich, but later in life he turns away from God.
- Solomon has seven hundred wives and three hundred concubines, or mistresses, even though God tells him not to do this.
- The women lead Solomon into worshiping false gods.
- God is furious with Solomon's defiance and promises that Solomon's dynasty will end.
- God lets Solomon's enemies trouble him for years.

Verse-atility: Who I am has little to do with fame and fortune.

POV: Recognize your weaknesses; stick with self-control.
Key Verse: "What good is it for a man to gain the whole world, and yet lose or forfeit his very self?" (Luke 9:25).

WHO WANTS TO BE FAMOUS? 1 Kings 10:23-25; 11:1-13 *(The Message)*
*(We've added a few of our own comments in **bold** below.)*

King Solomon was wiser and richer than all the kings of the earth—he surpassed them all. People came from all over the world to be with Solomon and drink in the wisdom God had given him. And everyone who came brought gifts—artifacts of gold and silver, fashionable robes and gowns, the latest in weapons, exotic spices, and horses and mules—parades of visitors, year after year.

. . . King Solomon was obsessed with women. **[A celeb's Bill of Rights?]** Pharaoh's daughter was only the first of the many foreign women he loved—Moabite, Ammonite, Edomite, Sidonian, and Hittite. He took them from the surrounding pagan nations of which God had clearly warned Israel, "You must not marry them; they'll seduce you into infatuations with their gods." Solomon fell in love with them anyway, refusing to give them up. He had seven hundred royal wives and three hundred concubines—a thousand women in all! **[. . . hitting bottom and starting to dig . . .]** And they did seduce him away from God. As Solomon grew older, his wives beguiled him with their alien gods and he became unfaithful—he didn't stay true to his God as his father David had done. Solomon took up with Ashtoreth, the whore goddess of the Sidonians, and Molech, the horrible god of the Ammonites.

Solomon openly defied God; he did not follow in his father David's footsteps. He went on to build a sacred shrine to Chemosh, the horrible god of Moab, and to Molech, the horrible god of the Ammonites, on a hill just east of Jerusalem. He built similar shrines for all his foreign wives, who then polluted the countryside with the smoke and stench of their sacrifices. **[Talk about eco-unfriendly actions . . .]**

God was furious with Solomon for abandoning the God of Israel, the God who had twice appeared to him and had so clearly commanded him not to fool around with other gods. Solomon faithlessly disobeyed God's orders.

God said to Solomon, "Since this is the way it is with you, that you have no intention of keeping faith with me and doing what I have commanded, **[here is my judgment:]** I'm going to rip the kingdom from you and hand it over to someone else. But out of respect for your father David I won't do it in your lifetime. It's your son who will pay. I'll rip it right out of his grasp. **[An unintended consequence.]** Even then I won't take it all; I'll leave him one tribe in honor of my servant David and out of respect for my chosen city Jerusalem."

6

The Trickmeister

Director's Commentary

NOW SHOWING: **The Trickmeister**

FROM THE BIBLE: Elisha tricks the Arameans (2 Kings 6:8-23).

RATED PG–13 FOR: ambush with intent to kidnap; life-and-death anxiety

POV: You're not alone—God lives in the world. You don't need to solve every problem by yourself.

KEY VERSE: "Don't be afraid. . . . Those who are with us are more than those who are with them" (2 Kings 6:16).

The Lesson	Time	What you'll do . . .	How you'll do it . . .	What you'll need . . .
Take 1: Preview	15 to 20 minutes	Start off your lesson by introducing the theme with a relational, creative activity.	Option 1: Students act out "Got Help?" drama and discuss it.	3 photocopies of the "Got Help?" script (pp. 86, 87); markers, group journal supplies (*Optional:* items from your prop box, which can include, for the actors: schoolbooks or 2 backpacks, 2 basketballs, 2 water bottles; movie snacks for your audience)
			Option 2: Students watch a DVD version of "Got Help?" and discuss it. Or, choose to do both.	*Dark and Disturbing Stories from the Bible DVD*, TV and DVD player; markers, group journal supplies
Take 2: Feature Presentation	15 to 20 minutes	Dive into the Bible story and explore it together.	Small group and large group discussion	Photocopies of **Outtakes** (p. 88); medium to large cardboard boxes, colorful markers *Optional:* Bibles
Take 3: Critics' Corner	15 to 20 minutes	Help your students grasp God's point of view and wrap things up with a fun team-building activity.	Discussion, game, and prayer	Photocopies of **Outtakes** (p. 88); group journal, markers; carpet squares or newspaper sheets, ink pad, wet wipes

WHY IS THIS PG-13 STORY IN THE BIBLE?

Elijah, Elisha—it gets confusing. Elijah, the great prophet who's taken to heaven in a chariot of fire, leaves Elisha to carry on the work of being God's great prophet of that time. Active for fifty years, Elisha sees the rule of several kings. The biblical record shows him to be a gutsy guy through whom God works miracles both in the lives of individual needs and in a nation that is in crisis.

In 2 Kings 6, Israel is involved in border clashes with Aram. The king of Aram plans various military maneuvers and, repeatedly, Elisha sends word to the king of Israel (probably Joram) to avoid the place where Aram is planning an ambush. The king of Aram interrogates his officers, and they tell him the snitch is Elisha—who gets his information straight from God, not a human spy. The king of Aram's next planned move is to break the cycle by capturing Elisha. If Elisha is stowed away somewhere, he won't be able to send word to the king. Aram's forces surround Dothan, the city where Elisha is staying.

Elisha's servant sees a circle of horses and chariots surrounding the city—and panics. Elisha sees something completely different. God opens the servant's eyes to see a second ring of horses and chariots—all made of fire! With this vision of the spiritual realm, Elisha knows where the real power lies. Then God answers Elisha's prayer to blind the oncoming troops to prevent them from seeing what's literally right in front of them: though they're looking for Elisha, they don't know they've found him! He promises to lead them to the man they're looking for, and they go with him into the heart of Samaria, where Israel's king waits.

One could argue that what Elisha says is technically true, because the soldiers are looking for him and he's there. Clearly, though, it's a trap. So what is the real point of what happens? A heavenly army protects Elisha; God answers Elisha's prayers on the spot; the king of Aram fails, the enemy army is captured, and Israel is secure. None of that happens by human effort, but rather because God does it. The king of Israel can't take credit for military

> **Connecting with Community**
> Log on to www.darkand disturbing.com to connect with other ministries:
> - Check out a sample video of other students in action.
> - Share with other leaders at the PG-13 forum about what's working in your ministry, what's not, or how you used *Dark and Disturbing* or *Shocking and Scandalous* this week.
> - Or ask for input about other aspects of middle school ministry.

strategy. The credit goes to God. Israel's security is anchored in God, who is Lord over every detail of life.

This story will help middle schoolers realize God is powerfully present in this world. And in times of crisis, they are not alone.

Take It to Your Students

Here are some key points in this lesson for your students:

- It's OK to ask for help.
- God is present, even when you don't see or feel him. He cares.
- You don't have to solve every problem by yourself. ✗

The Trickmeister: The Lesson

Take 1: Preview (15 to 20 minutes)

Setup: This activity will set up the day's Bible story in a relational way as students perform a skit in which a preteen struggles with his transition to middle school.

Set design: Create a relaxed atmosphere for *Preview.* Ask students to sit on the floor in a circle on pillows, seat cushions, or colorful mats. The drama will be performed in the middle. Popcorn or movie snacks will help set a movie mood.

Makeup and effects: For today's drama, consider having students select props and costumes from your one-size-fits-all prop box.

Props: Supplies for the journal option you've chosen, markers; 3 copies of the "Got Help?" skit (pp. 86, 87); or the *Dark and Disturbing Stories from the Bible DVD* with TV and DVD player; or choose both activities

Optional for the drama: items from your prop box, which can include schoolbooks or 2 backpacks, 2 basketballs, 2 water bottles; movie snacks for your audience

QUIET ON THE SET

To launch the lesson:

- Welcome everyone to the group. Use first names or preferred nicknames and introduce visitors. After your students have had some time to socialize, pull them in and have them get comfortable.

- Go over your Rules of Engagement, if needed. (See the Rules of Engagement suggestions on p. 6 for more information.)
- Review the journaling component you've chosen for your group. (See Create a Group Journal on p. 10 for more information.)

ACTION

Either have students perform the "Got Help?" skit, watch "Got Help?" on the *Dark and Disturbing Stories from the Bible DVD*, or do both. If you choose to have students perform the skit live, give copies of the "Got

> **Option:** If you want, make a video of your students' live performance. Play it back for the group, the group and parents, or maybe the entire church.

Help?" handout to student actors and have them prep by reading through their parts a time or two. Also invite the actors to rummage through the prop box for items to enhance the performance.

(Note: The script in this lesson has an extra role not on the DVD video. This script contains narrator's lines. An extra opportunity for one of your kids to get up front!)

PLAY BACK

Spend time reflecting on "Got Help?" with your group by using the discussion suggestions below. Don't edit your students' responses; allow them to discuss freely. Also, have a volunteer record the group's impressions through the group journal method you've chosen. Jot "Got Help?" and today's date at the top of the journal entry. Give every student the opportunity to comment or to journal, even if it's just to initial in agreement with the posted entries.

Can you relate with Mike? For many preteens, the shift to middle school means high anxiety with five-minute transition periods between classes, lockers, tough homework assignments and, of course, a new social order.

Use these questions to get a group discussion going:

- **Why do you think Mike feels the need to go it alone? Are there some feelings he just can't share? Explain.**
- **What are some of the reasons why bullies pick on others? Share your ideas.** *(They want to give some appearance of power and control. They're insecure themselves and have no other way to express it.)*
- **Can anything help Mike and kids like him? Explain.** *(Don't be afraid to ask for help. Realize plenty of other kids struggle with the challenges of middle school.)*

- What concerns did you face in your first weeks at a new school? What's in your "anxiety closet" that you feel comfortable sharing?

Great and honest discussion, guys. The choice to go it alone has Mike in a tight fix. Today's PG-13 movie shines the spotlight on a masterful leader who is singled out but who never goes it alone. Ambush and deceit, interrogation and intel from the highest source bring the heat in today's flick, *The Trickmeister.* ✘

Take 2: Feature Presentation   (15 to 20 minutes)

Setup: Your students will take a close look at the story of Elisha and the Arameans and discuss God's presence and action in the world.

Props: Photocopies of **Outtakes** (p. 88); medium or large cardboard boxes (one per small group), colorful markers

Optional: Bibles

QUIET ON THE SET

Pass out copies of **Outtakes**, one per student. Optional: Have students grab their own Bibles.

ACTION

Use **Outtakes** to introduce and teach the Bible story. First, briefly introduce the **Cast** and make sure your students know who's who. Next, use **Movie Trailer** to cover the highlights of the Bible background and story. Then, read the Bible story (2 Kings 6:8-23) out loud from **Outtakes** or have a volunteer read it. If you prefer, ask students to read the passage aloud from their own Bibles.

PLAY BACK

Break into two or more small teams for discussion with an older teen or adult leader for each group. Assign half the teams to explore the actions of the king of Aram and his soldiers (Team Talk 1, below) and the other half to dig into the actions of Elisha and his servant (Team Talk 2). Remind group leaders to be ready to enhance discussion with insights from **Why Is This PG-13 Story in the Bible?** (p. 77).

Give each group a medium to large cardboard box and a bunch of colorful markers. Have students discuss and write about the motivations they see in the story characters while decorating their box to look like a chariot of fire by using word art. Examples: to put wheels on the chariot, students can write words in circles with a black marker. They also can write in straight lines in brown for the horses' reins or use orange and wavy lines to look like flames.

This story is full of incredible twists and turns. Let's view today's cast.

Team Talk 1: Get into the heads of the king of Aram and his soldiers.

- **What's bothering the king of Aram so much he can't stand it?** (*The king of Israel always seems to know what he's planning; it makes him look ridiculous.*)
- **What does the king of Aram think his big problem is? What do you think his big problem is?** (*He's got to find a way around this military problem! His real trouble is that he underestimates the power of Israel's God.*)
- **How would you describe the king of Aram's problem-solving strategy?** (*Conquer and crush; win by power.*)
- **How are the Aramean soldiers caught in the middle of things?** (*They're following instructions, no matter what they might think. They become pawns in Elisha's response to the situation.*)

Team Talk 2: Get into the heads of Elisha and his servant.

- **What does Elisha's servant see when there's a problem? What does Elisha see?** (*This appears to be a terrifying situation! God is in control!*)
- **Step into the sandals of Elisha's servant. What would you feel or think if you suddenly saw that angel army?** (*That's incredible! What else have I been missing all this time?!*)
- **How would you describe Elisha's problem-solving strategy? What are Elisha's biggest problem-solving tools?** (*Trust God; be wise; pray; ask God for insight. He has confidence that the spiritual world is true and in force because he saw the angel army.*)
- **What does Elisha's decision at the end of this story say about him?** (*He knows ultimately it's all in God's hands. He doesn't have to take drastic action to solve*

> Remember that even if you've got a small-sized group of eight or ten participants, it's still important to have students break up into Team Talk small groups so they can deepen friendships and freely share their thoughts and ideas about the Bible story. But if you've got just six students or less, it's probably best to go ahead and discuss both sets of Team Talk questions together as one group.

the problem of the Arameans himself. He shows great mercy when it would have been easy to be vengeful. He gives glory to God, not himself.)

Bring the discussion teams back together. Briefly review what they talked about by reading and admiring the word art on their cardboard chariots.

Continue your discussion as a large group by asking questions like:

- **What surprised you the most in this story?** *(The Aramean army would be defeated in this way. That Elisha stays so calm through the entire situation.)*
- **What does this story teach us about solving problems?** *(Ultimately, trust God! Our solutions aren't at all what God's would be.)*
- **Why do you think this story is in the Bible?** *(This is a good opportunity to remind students of the Key Verse: "Don't be afraid. . . . Those who are with us are more than those who are with them" [2 Kings 6:16].)*

Military secrets were being leaked. The king of Aram ordered a top-secret maneuver to plug the leak. His plan: kill Elisha. The wise prophet drew strength from a fundamental belief: *I am not alone. I serve God. He will not abandon me when I need him most.*

Use these questions to prompt more large-group discussion:

- **If Elisha were going to express doubt, at what part of the story could it have happened?**
- **What main idea from the story does the Key Verse remind us of?**
- **How can this story encourage you the next time you face a big problem?**

Problems can feel overwhelming at times. When that happens, remind yourself: *I'm not alone. God is in my life and I have family and friends who care about me. I don't have to solve every problem by myself.* ✗

Take 3: Critics' Corner   (15 to 20 minutes)

Setup: Reinforce the points you want your students to take away from today's lesson.

Props: **Outtakes** (p. 88); group journal with entries from Take 1, markers; carpet squares or newspaper sheets, ink pad, wet wipes

QUIET ON THE SET

Grab the group journal and together review the "Got Help?" entries recorded during Take 1. Ask your group for a thumbs-up if they believe they have a good read on Mike's concerns.

ACTION

Consider the POV

Draw a large thumbprint in the group journal to symbolize the uniqueness of each student in your class and God's loving care for individual concerns. Create wavy lines to write on, mimicking the skin ridges on a real fingerprint.

Ask the group:

- **Think about some consequences for Mike if he doesn't ask for help. How might a new approach convince Mike to give things another try?** (*His year might get tougher and tougher and he might begin to really feel lost. Seeking help from his parents, teachers, a school counselor, or his coach can only help, not hurt.*)
- **What "next step" ideas do you have for Mike? List your ideas on the fingerprint.** (*Pray to God for direction; drop the word "failure" from any discussion; request homework help; speak up and don't put up with bullies; step up and help other kids who need it.*)

Re-title the page by replacing the question mark with an exclamation point to read "Got Help!" Then have the group repeat today's **POV** as a team: *We're not alone—God lives in the world. We don't need to solve every problem by ourselves.* Invite students to affirm their belief in God's help in their lives and in the POV statement by having them press their thumbs onto an ink pad, then fingerprint the group journal page. Pass out wet wipes for clean up.

Understand God's Truth

Elisha's servant sees the enemy's chariots and panics. Elisha sees God's power at work. The difference in outlook is striking. As believers, we have a friend in high places! Like Elisha, we shouldn't hesitate to ask for help at every turn.

Ask the group:

- **What have we learned from today's story?** (*Even in a crisis, we're not alone; our security is anchored in God.*)

Option: If you want, have students form pairs to talk about these three questions. A one-on-one setting will enable them to open up and be more candid with each other.

- Imagine that a friend asked you these questions: "Do you really think God is your friend? Does he really care about you and your life?" How would you answer?
- What's one situation in your life right now in which it's a comfort to know that God is with you—that you're not alone?

Once trapped, King Aram's troops are doomed. The death they sought for Elisha is now staring them in the face. To give God the glory, Elisha feeds his would-be killers and sends them home. It's a wise prophet statement from a practice-what-you-preach holy man.

Teamwork

Sometimes problems loom so large that we lose sight of a critical truth: God lives in the world. He's your protector and friend. Whatever concerns you concerns him. No secrets. No games.

We can help each other keep this truth front and center by reminding each other of God's presence, his power, and his trustworthiness. Commit to God and each other this week.

PLAY BACK

Wrap up the meeting with a team-building game that helps students reflect on cooperation to resolve a difficult situation. Close in prayer.

It Takes a Village

Needed: carpet squares or newspaper sheets (1 for each player plus 1 extra per team)
Goal: Cooperate and use "stepping-stones" to reach dry land.

How to Play:

Determine a start and finish line for this game, the two lines at least fifty feet apart. Form five-player teams (or however best your group divides) and have teams line up single file along the "river's edge" (the start line). Teams must work together, using their squares as stepping-stones to cross the river. The team must cross bringing *all* the stepping-stones and team members along. Play proceeds with the last team member in line picking up the last stepping-

stone and passing it to the front, where it is
laid down again and the team moves forward.
Players must not touch the "water" (the floor)
or they risk a horrible fate (drowning; being
eaten by crocodiles)! If any player touches
the "water" with any part of his or her body,

Option: For more challenging
play, decrease the stepping-
stones by one less for every
five players. Add obstacles like
tables and chairs to navigate
under and over.

that player's team must return to the riverbank and try crossing again. The first
team to successfully navigate these troubled waters wins.

After the game, say: **Great job! You needed each other to come through as a
team. We try but we can't always make it on our own. Thankfully, we have God,
our Father, who lives in the world, and we have each other—so we never have to.**

Close with Prayer

Ask your students to look at **Outtakes** again
and repeat today's **Key Verse:** "Don't be
afraid. . . . Those who are with us are more
than those who are with them" (2 Kings

Verse-atility: *Release fear. God
is near.*

6:16). Then point out the teen-friendly *Verse-atility* to keep God's truth front
and center in your students' lives this week: *Release fear. God is near.* If time
permits, jot the verse in the group journal and have everyone initial it.

Can you hear me now? God answers Elisha's prayers on the spot in today's
story! Listen for prayer requests. Pray for immediate, in-the-moment support
and protection for every member in your group, present or not. ✗

Got Help?

Characters:
NARRATOR
DAMON: a sixth-grade guy
MIKE: a sixth-grade guy
Scene: DAMON and MIKE are walking home from after-school basketball practice.
Prop Suggestions: Select any props or costumes you want from the prop box. Also, if you want, use things like schoolbooks or 2 backpacks, 2 basketballs, water bottles (or just pretend!).

SCRIPT

(DAMON and MIKE are walking down a residential street, heading home following after-school basketball practice.)

NARRATOR:
Damon is having a great start in middle school. But his best friend, Mike, is finding it hard to adjust. They're talking small talk and taking it easy as they head home—when Mike begins to open up.

DAMON:
. . . That question, where it asked about the pilgrims? That was pretty easy.

MIKE:
Are you serious? . . . The only thing I've got down is homeroom—and my locker combo.

DAMON:
Yeah, homeroom is *the* best time to chill. I love how Miss Grange gives us candy at the end of the day.

MIKE:
(groaning) Ah man, pre-algebra is making my brain hurt. I mean, homework every night . . . and notebook checks!?

DAMON:
(laughing, still not getting his friend's pain) I remember this one time, I was walking across the parking lot, and I ran right into a hall room security guard. When have we ever had to deal with that before?

MIKE:
Computer, Spanish, third-period lunch. It's crazy. There is *way* too much to keep track of.

DAMON:
(twirling basketball) I like band. Health's OK. But you've gotta remember: there's always basketball!

MIKE:
You're lucky your locker isn't on the other side of the building. I've already gotten a write-up for being late to class. *(shaking head)* I'm just trying to get through the day. I feel like I'm failing at everything.

DAMON:
You're not failing, dude. And besides—you kicked everybody's butt at basketball today.

(MIKE stops, shrugs. He's not sure what to say.)

DAMON:
(now working to cheer up his friend) **Ah, c'mon. Why don't you try to get extra credit? Or get help from a counselor? You're not alone in this, Mike.**

MIKE:
See a counselor? You're kidding, right?

DAMON:
Well, Mr. C is a good guy. And asking for help from him is not a crime.

MIKE:
Well . . . schoolwork's only part of it.

DAMON:
Whataya mean, Mike?

MIKE:
(now starting to look a little embarrassed) **A few of the older kids mess with me at school, OK? . . . And my stuff.**

DAMON:
(surprised) **Well—why didn't you tell me this before?**

MIKE:
(definitely feeling uncomfortable) **Never mind . . .**

DAMON:
(now he really wants to help) **Ah, c'mon Mike. You don't have to . . . You don't have to take it.**

MIKE:
(starting to turn and head for home) **I can handle it. It's . . . It's OK.** *(Mike doesn't sound too convinced.)* **See ya.** *(He turns and runs down the street.)*

DAMON:
(Shouting after Mike) **Mike . . . wait! C'mon dude!** *(Mike runs off and Damon starts after him, but then decides to let him have his space.)*

NARRATOR:
The school year doesn't look good if Mike can't get it together. What should he do? What would you do if you were Mike's friend?

(Skit ends; actors join the rest of the group.)

Outtakes

CAST

King of Aram: at war with Israel
King of Israel: at war with Aram
Aramean army: sent by king to capture Elisha
Elisha: God's prophet to Israel
Servant: helps Elisha

MOVIE TRAILER

- Every time the king of Aram plans a new attack, the king of Israel finds out.
- Elisha is the one who knows the king's plans—because God tells him.
- The king of Aram sends troops to get Elisha; Elisha's servant is very afraid.
- At Elisha's request, God opens the servant's eyes and he sees an army of heaven's angels protecting them.
- Elisha asks God to make the troops blind, then the prophet leads them to a trap in Samaria.
- The king of Israel wants to kill the troops, but Elisha feeds them a feast instead.

Verse-atility: Release fear. God is near.

POV: You're not alone—God lives in the world. You don't need to solve every problem by yourself.
Key Verse: "Don't be afraid. . . . Those who are with us are more than those who are with them" (2 Kings 6:16).

THE TRICKMEISTER 2 Kings 6:8-23 *(The Message) (We've added a few of our own comments in **bold** below.)*

One time when the king of Aram was at war with Israel, after consulting with his officers, he said, "At such and such a place I want an ambush set."

The Holy Man **[that would be Elisha]** sent a message to the king of Israel: "Watch out when you're passing this place, because Aram has set an ambush there."

So the king of Israel sent word concerning the place of which the Holy Man had warned him. This kind of thing happened all the time. **[That's one powerful prophet.]**

The king of Aram was furious over all this. He called his officers together and said, "Tell me, who is leaking information to the king of Israel? Who is the spy in our ranks?"

But one of his men said, "No, my master, dear king. It's not any of us. It's Elisha the prophet in Israel. He tells the king of Israel everything you say, even what you whisper in your bedroom."

The king said, "Go and find out where he is. I'll send someone and capture him."

The report came back, "He's in Dothan."

Then he dispatched horses and chariots, an impressive fighting force. They came by night and surrounded the city.

Early in the morning a servant of the Holy Man got up and went out. Surprise! Horses and chariots surrounding the city! The young man exclaimed, "Oh, master! What shall we do?"

He said, "Don't worry about it—there are more on our side than on their side."

Then Elisha prayed, "O God, open his eyes and let him see."

The eyes of the young man were opened and he saw. A wonder! The whole mountainside full of horses and chariots of fire surrounding Elisha!

When the Arameans attacked, Elisha prayed to God, "Strike these people blind!" And God struck them blind, just as Elisha said.

Then Elisha called out to them, "Not that way! Not this city! Follow me and I'll lead you to the man you're looking for." And he led them into Samaria **[Israel's capital]**.

As they entered the city, Elisha prayed, "O God, open their eyes so they can see where they are." God opened their eyes. They looked around—they were trapped in Samaria!

When the king of Israel saw them, he said to Elisha, "Father, shall I massacre the lot?"

"Not on your life!" said Elisha. "You didn't lift a hand to capture them, and now you're going to kill them? No sir, make a feast for them and send them back to their master." **[Catch and release!]**

So he prepared a huge feast for them. After they ate and drank their fill he dismissed them. Then they returned home to their master. The raiding bands of Aram didn't bother Israel anymore. **[Ya think?]**

7

Face-off

Director's Commentary

NOW SHOWING: *Face-off*

FROM THE BIBLE: King Uzziah shows contempt for God and gets leprosy (2 Chronicles 26:9-23).

RATED PG-13 FOR: disturbing images (facial disfigurement)

POV: There's more to life than being a bossy know-it-all; check your attitude.

KEY VERSE: "Do not think of yourself more highly than you ought, but rather think of yourself with sober judgment" (Romans 12:3).

The Lesson	Time	What you'll do . . .	How you'll do it . . .	What you'll need . . .
Take 1: Preview	15 to 20 minutes	Start off your lesson by introducing the theme with a relational, creative activity.	Option 1: Students act out "We the People" drama and discuss it.	4 copies of the "We the People" script (pp. 99, 100); group journal supplies, markers (*Optional:* prop box; schoolbooks or backpacks, paper, pen and clipboard, campaign buttons or poster; movie snacks for your audience)
			Option 2: Students watch a DVD version of "We the People." Or, choose to do both	*Dark and Disturbing Stories from the Bible DVD*, TV, DVD player; group journal supplies, markers
Take 2: Feature Presentation	15 to 20 minutes	Dive into the Bible story and explore it together.	Small group and large group discussion	Photocopies of **Outtakes** (p. 101); paper grocery sacks, newspaper, markers *Optional:* Bibles
Take 3: Critics' Corner	15 to 20 minutes	Help your students grasp God's point of view and wrap things up with a fun team-building activity.	Discussion, game, and prayer	Group journal; **Outtakes** (p. 101); Bibles; candy with holes (as in the Life Savers brand), pasta wheels or small twisted pretzels, drinking straws or coffee stirrers

WHY IS THIS PG-13 STORY IN THE BIBLE?

Why does a good king suddenly lose his way?

Uzziah ruled Judah for fifty-two years. The well-known prophets Amos and Hosea were active during his reign, and Isaiah's famous vision of God happened at the end of Uzziah's kingship. In this period of history, God's people were divided into two kingdoms: Israel to the north and Judah to the south. The spirituality of kings varied widely, and while Judah did have a few righteous kings, the northern kingdom of Israel had virtually none. Uzziah, in the south, was one of the few kings who "did what was right in the eyes of the Lord," and did so "just as his father Amaziah had done" (2 Chronicles 26:4). God blessed Uzziah's efforts.

Where his father had tried to gain additional territory, Uzziah focused on solidifying his base, modernizing the military, and expanding the agricultural network of the nation. He experienced significant military success against the Israelites' old enemies, the Philistines and Ammonites, and brought irrigation to thirsty fields.

Uzziah was rich, successful, popular—so what went wrong? The problem came when Uzziah arrogantly decided that he, as king, had the right to be priest if he wanted to. Wrong! God had established separate roles for kings and priests. The temple work was to be done by the descendents of Aaron who were given special dedication to this ministry. Not just anyone could walk into the temple and light the incense. Not even the king.

But one day Uzziah tried to do just that. Azariah and eighty other priests confront him and insist he leave the temple. He doesn't. So God steps in. Uzziah's face breaks out with a skin disease. Traditional translations call it leprosy—but this could be a description of a wide range of skin conditions. It's not important specifically what it is; the point is the disease makes Uzziah unclean. This means he has no business being in the temple at all, even to worship. Uzziah now panics and knows he has to hightail it out of there. Too late! Pride becomes his undoing.

The disease lasts for the rest of the king's life, disqualifying him from temple worship and forcing him to turn over kingdom rule to his son.

This Bible story will illustrate for students that a big head serves to give you one thing: tunnel vision. Acting like a tyrant never helps—attitude counts.

Take It to Your Students

Here are some key points for your students in this lesson:

- It's one thing to be proud of what you accomplish. It's something else to think that it puts you above God's law.
- Too much success can be dangerous; watch yourself.
- Doing an attitude check upfront will save you a painful attitude adjustment later.

Face-off: The Lesson

Take 1: Preview (15 to 20 minutes)

Setup: This activity will set up the day's Bible story in a relational way as students watch a skit about a student council campaign and a not-so-hot attitude.

Set design: Create a relaxed atmosphere for *Preview.* Ask students to sit on the floor in a circle on pillows, seat cushions, or colorful mats. The drama will be performed in the middle. Popcorn or movie snacks will help set a movie mood.

Makeup and effects: For today's drama, consider having students select props and costumes from your one-size-fits-all prop box.

Props: Supplies for the journal option you've chosen, markers; 4 copies of the "We the People" script (pp. 99, 100), or the *Dark and Disturbing Stories from the Bible DVD* with TV and DVD player—or choose to do both activities *Optional:* items from your prop box; schoolbooks or backpacks, paper, pen and clipboard, campaign buttons or poster; movie snacks for your audience

QUIET ON THE SET

To launch the lesson:

- Welcome everyone to the group. Use first names or preferred nicknames and introduce visitors. After your students have had some time to socialize, pull them in and have them get comfortable.

- Go over your Rules of Engagement, if needed. (See the Rules of Engagement suggestions on p. 6 for more information.)
- Review the journaling component you've chosen for your group. (See Create a Group Journal on p. 10 for more information.)

Option: If you want, make a video of your students' live performance. Play it back for the group, the group and parents, or maybe the entire church.

ACTION

Either have students perform the "We the People" skit, watch "We the People" on the *Dark and Disturbing Stories from the Bible DVD*, or do both. If you choose to have students perform the skit live, give copies of "We the People" to your student actors and have them prep by reading through their parts a few times. Also, invite actors to rummage through the prop box for items to enhance their performance.

PLAY BACK

Spend time reflecting on "We the People" with your group by using the discussion suggestions below. Don't edit your students' responses—allow them to discuss freely.

Have a volunteer jot "We the People" and today's date on your group journal, then record the group's impressions. Give every student the opportunity to comment or to journal, even if it's just to initial in agreement with the entries.

A know-it-all attitude shuts out and shuts down others, leaving little room for discussion.

Use these questions to get the discussion going:

- How would you define "having an attitude" in your own words?
- Do the words *bigheaded* or *conceited* apply to David? Why or why not?
- How is being confident different from having an attitude? Explain your views.
- How might David's attitude reflect on Makayla?
- What would you do in a similar situation?

A poor attitude is a dare of sorts—one that seeks to challenge and come out on top. Today's PG-13 presentation stars a stunningly egotistical leader of the royal pack. Rich and revered, he decides that rules no longer apply to him. It's

My-way-or-the-highway meets The Lawgiver in a real showdown, in *Face-off*, up next. X

Take 2: Feature Presentation (15 to 20 minutes)

Setup: Your students will take a close look at the story of Uzziah and discuss the dangers of out-of-control pride.

Props: Photocopies of **Outtakes** (p. 101); paper grocery sacks, newspaper, markers
Optional: Bibles

QUIET ON THE SET

Pass out copies of **Outtakes**, one per student. Optional: Have students grab their own Bibles.

ACTION

Use **Outtakes** to introduce and teach the Bible story. First, briefly introduce the **Cast** and make sure your students know who's who. Next, use **Movie Trailer** to cover the highlights of the Bible background and story. Then read the Bible story (2 Chronicles 26:9-23) out loud from **Outtakes** or have a volunteer read it. If you prefer, ask students to read the passage aloud from their Bibles.

PLAY BACK

Divide your group into two or more small teams for discussion. Assign half the teams to explore Uzziah's actions (Team Talk 1, below) and the other half to explore the priests' actions (Team Talk 2). Remind group leaders to be ready to enhance discussion with insights from **Why Is This PG-13 Story in the Bible?** (p. 90).

Give each group a paper grocery sack, newspaper, and markers. Tell each team to stuff a grocery sack with newspaper and then sculpt their creation into the shape of a "swelled head." As students discuss the motivations they see in the story characters, they can write their observations on the head.

> *What's the big deal?* Either in the large group or in small groups, explain that God had given his people strict instructions that only priests were to perform certain acts of worship, including burning incense. These temple regulations were common knowledge—clear to everybody. What might at first seem "so what?" to us would have been a serious offense at the time the story took place.

Uzziah's disrespect for God is astounding. Desperate for God-power, the king fearlessly—and foolishly—steps over the line, a boundary that God had clearly drawn.

Team Talk 1: Get into the head of King Uzziah.

- **What accomplishments do you think led to Uzziah's big head?** *(Military and agricultural success; being the king)*
- **"I'm not God, but I play one on TV!" When Uzziah goes for the censer, what attitude comes into sharp focus?** *(Contempt for God; he can do whatever he wants; pride; arrogance; hunger for power)*
- **Leprosy was a dreaded disease with no cure in Bible times. How would having this disease be an attack on Uzziah's pride and power?** *(You can explain that leprosy, rarely seen in North America today, was a chronic infectious skin disease caused by bacteria. If left untreated, the disease caused swollen and blistered skin lesions leading to permanent damage to the skin, arms, and legs.) (Having the disease would make Uzziah humble and vulnerable—and an outcast.)*
- **What price did Uzziah pay for his prideful grab for power?** *(He had the disease the rest of his life; he was forbidden from visiting the temple; he had to give up ruling the nation; he was kept from burial in the royal graveyard.)*

Team Talk 2: Get into the heads of the priests.

- **Eighty-one priests struggle to get Uzziah out of the temple. Why so many?** *(What Uzziah tries to do is so extreme they're all appalled.)*
- **How do they try to get him to leave?** *(Tell him straight out. Appeal to his sense of right and wrong.)*
- **How well do these methods work?** *(Not very. It takes God's intervention.)*
- **If you had been one of the priests, what would you have said to Uzziah?**
- **What finally happens to get Uzziah out of the temple's incense altar area?** *(Uzziah breaks out in disease. The priests know that God is present and involved.)*

Bring the discussion groups back together. Briefly review results of discussions by reading what students wrote on the paper bag heads. Continue your discussion as a large group by asking:

- **How does this story show pride's good** *("I'm a success!")* **and bad** *("I'm a success at any cost")* **sides?**
- **Why do you think it's hard to see selfish pride at work in ourselves even though it's usually easy for us to see it in others?**

• **Why do you think this story about pride and disease is in the Bible?** *(This is a good opportunity to remind students of the Key Verse: "Do not think of yourself more highly than you ought, but rather think of yourself with sober judgment" [Romans 12:3]).*

Uzziah went on a head trip, and initial efforts to rein him in had no effect. God's power strikes, leaving a decisive and disfiguring blow. Uzziah soon gets the point.

Use these key questions to prompt more large-group discussion:

• **Name the places where Uzziah could have made a choice that would have changed how the story turned out.** *(He could have decided not to enter the temple's incense area at all; he could have immediately left when the priests first told him to.)*
• **How does today's Key Verse illustrate the main point of this story?**
• **How does this story challenge you and your sense of pride? Explain.**

Success is a powerful feeling, and this isn't necessarily a bad thing. But as today's story shows, success can lead to a swelled head. There's more to life—and success, for that matter—than being a bossy know-it-all. Keep your attitude in check. ✖

Take 3: Critics' Corner   (15 to 20 minutes)

Setup: Reinforce the points you want your students to take away from today's lesson.
Props: Group journal with entries from Take 1; **Outtakes** handout (p. 101);
  Bibles; candy with holes (as in the Life Savers brand), pasta wheels or small
  twisted pretzels, drinking straws or coffee stirrers

QUIET ON THE SET

Grab the group journal and ask students to review the "We the People" entries recorded earlier.

ACTION

Consider the POV

Ask the group:

• **What are some effects of having a bad attitude?** *(Others will see me as pessimistic, discouraging, angry, judgmental, or exclusive; it shuts down group* *conversation and creativity; I can lose friends; having one can interfere with my long-term goals.)*

- **Attitude adjustment: What should Makayla do to get David back in check?** *(State firmly that his attitude is unattractive, unreasonable, and unacceptable; resolve not to put up with David's behavior or self-serving requests.)*

Ask students to read Matthew 5:3-10 from their Bibles and discover the "Great Eight Attitude Tips" of all time! Jot a condensed version of these bedrock teachings of Jesus in the group journal. Then ask:

- **Which one of these attitudes stands out to you as an important one for your life? Why?**
- **What attitude in your life could you replace with one of these teachings? Share why.**

Draw students' attention to the **POV** on the **Outtakes** page and repeat it together: *There's more to life than being a bossy know-it-all; check your attitude.*

Understand God's Truth

King Uzziah squandered his power and sought a position he had no business coveting. When he did, God decided to step in. A little humility would have gone a long way in keeping this influential ruler healthy, wealthy, and wise.

Ask the group:

- **Uzziah was rich and popular. Would you like these things too? Be honest! Why or why not?** *(Thoughts for your students: if your answer is "sure!" do a background check first. How's your attitude? Fulfill your heart's desires with God in mind first.)*
- **What have we learned from today's story?** *(Point out today's Key Verse: "Do not think of yourself more highly than you ought, but rather think of yourself with sober judgment" [Romans 12:3].)*

God blessed Uzziah, and then came a major setback. With increased power, Uzziah eventually became arrogant, resisted rules, and became unfaithful to his maker. Contempt is no match for our amazing God.

Teamwork

You knew it all along. A bad attitude pushes buttons and invades boundaries. And that will not be us! Let's work together to help each other replace attitude with gratitude and be humble leaders this week.

PLAY BACK

Wrap up the meeting with a team-building game. Then close with prayer.

Candy-gram

Needed: small-holed candy (like the Life Savers brand), pasta wheels or small twist pretzels, drinking straws cut in half or coffee stirrers
Goal: Be the first team to successfully pass candy from player to player.

How to Play:

Form small game circles of eight to ten players each. Note: It's best if you do this activity in groups of all guys or all girls and not mixed genders. (If your group is small, a single circle will work too. Eliminate the competition element and just play for fun.)

Distribute half a drinking straw (or a whole stirrer) to each player. Ask players to place one end of the straw between their teeth, then close their mouths. Slide a single piece of candy onto the first player's straw. Do this for each team.

When you say "Go!", have teams pass candies from one player's straw to another's as quickly as possible. If candy drops, play starts over for that team. The first team to successfully pass the candy full circle (no hands allowed) wins. (If you want, you can extend the game by having teams pass the candy back around their circle in reverse.)

After the game, say: **Sometimes humble silence is the best way to go. Is there**

There's nothing like the power of laughter to build and strengthen relationships. Enjoy the silliness of this game! When your students have fun with one another, it serves as a powerful glue that helps them bond together.

Option: Have teams line up instead of forming circles. The first in line gets a roll (or portion) of holed candy; the last in line gets an extra drinking straw to hold. The first in line will pass the candy continually down the line (one piece after the other) while the last in line stacks it on the straw he or she holds. The first team to stack the holding straw full of candy wins.

someone you know who could use this friendly advice? How about yourself? The chat room is now open! (But don't use other people's names!)

Verse-atility: *I'll take a hard look at my attitude.*

Close with Prayer

To keep God's truth front and center in your students' lives this week, ask your group to repeat today's **Key Verse:** "Do not think of yourself more highly than you ought, but rather think of yourself with sober judgment" (Romans 12:3). Then point out this week's *Verse-atility*: *I'll take a hard look at my attitude.* If time permits, jot the verse in the group journal and have everyone initial it.

Listen for prayer requests. Pray for your group's courage and to live with a humble, God-honoring attitude and to resist the temptations of pride. ✘

We the People

Characters:
MAKAYLA and ASHLEY: two middle school girls
DAVID and JAKE: two middle school guys
Scene: The four friends have gathered in the school hallway to wait for the student council election results. ASHLEY is starting to take down some of the "Vote for Makayla!" posters.
Prop Suggestions: Select any props or costumes you want from the prop box. You might have things like pen and clipboard, campaign buttons or posters—or have your students just pretend!

SCRIPT

MAKAYLA:
(*nervous, but excited*) **This is killing me! I can't take it any longer!**

DAVID:
They'll announce the student council election results in (*pause to check hall clock*) **. . . fifteen minutes.**

ASHLEY:
I really hope you get it, Makayla.

JAKE:
Yeah, good luck, Vice President!

MAKAYLA:
Thanks guys. I'm really happy that I ran. I'm feeling really confident.

JAKE:
I really liked your speech. And high-speed Internet in the library? Needed!

DAVID:
(*tapping on Jake's shoulder, but loud enough for everyone to hear*) **Just so you know, Jake, uh, that was my idea.**

ASHLEY:
And you did a great job, David, with Makayla's campaign slogan. . . . (*ASHLEY and JAKE repeat in unison:*) **"In Makayla we trust! Vote you must!"**

DAVID:
I put together the whole package. Election posters. Cookie bags with Makayla's name on them. Cafeteria talk show . . .

MAKAYLA:
(*giving DAVID a nudge, starting to get a bit annoyed*) **I think my campaign has gone to your head.**

JAKE:
Yeah, David, you had some really good ideas, but Makayla sold it.

ASHLEY:
Makayla's people skills are amazing. She works well with the administration, and she was the council secretary last year.

JAKE:
And she's funny!

MAKAYLA:
(brightening, forgetting the tension; a smile comes to her face) **Why did the chicken cross the road? To vote for Makayla Matthews for Vice President! Yeah? . . .**

(collective groan from all three)

MAKAYLA:
It's easy being cheesy!

ASHLEY:
I'll vote for that!

DAVID:
Well, without me, she wouldn't be on top. That's all I'm saying.

ASHLEY:
Get a grip, David.

DAVID:
FYI, Ashley. I'm a football star at this school. You know it. I know it. I've got influence. But I want more. After Makayla's elected, she can return the favor.

MAKAYLA:
(very suspicious) **You're kidding me, right?**

JAKE:
Are you saying that . . . you volunteered to be her campaign manager, just . . . to get something for yourself?

DAVID:
(calmly) **I want the fundraising job on the social committee.**

MAKAYLA:
I can't do that! There are rules. You don't have any experience.

DAVID:
The eighth graders worship me. I'm a shoo-in. *(DAVID turns to walk off. As he does, he condescendingly pats MAKAYLA on the head.)* **Watch and learn, newbie. Watch and learn.**

ASHLEY:
Your ego is showing, David.

(The group watches as David strolls off.)

JAKE:
(dripping with sarcasm) **There goes the power behind the throne.**

MAKAYLA:
(now seriously upset) **Unbelievable!**

(Skit ends. Actors join the rest of the group.)

Outtakes

CAST

Uzziah: king of Judah (part of God's people), a high-achiever king
Azariah: temple priest
Eighty priests: loyal to the laws of God

MOVIE TRAILER

- In the early years of his rule, Uzziah pleased God and did a lot of great work.
- But Uzziah becomes prideful and decides the rules don't apply to him.
- One day he goes into the temple to do a job only the priests are supposed to do.
- Azariah and eighty other priests try to talk sense into him, but Uzziah won't listen.
- A skin disease breaks out on the king's face. Now he's ready to get out of the temple— because he knows God did this to him.
- Uzziah has the disease for the rest of his life and can never go in the temple again.
- His life ends in dishonor.

Verse–atility: I'll take a hard look at my attitude.

POV: There's more to life than being a bossy know-it-all; check your attitude.
Key Verse: "Do not think of yourself more highly than you ought, but rather think of yourself with sober judgment" (Romans 12:3).

FACE-OFF

2 Chronicles 26:9-23 *(The Message)*
(We've added a few of our own comments in **bold** below.)

Uzziah constructed defense towers in Jerusalem at the Corner Gate, the Valley Gate, and at the corner of the wall. He also built towers and dug cisterns out in the country. He had herds of cattle down in the foothills and out on the plains, had farmers and vinedressers at work in the hills and fields—he loved growing things.

On the military side, Uzziah had a well-prepared army ready to fight. . . . Uzziah had them well-armed with shields, spears, helmets, armor, bows, and slingshots. He also installed the latest in military technology on the towers and corners of Jerusalem for shooting arrows and hurling stones. He became well known for all this—a famous king **[a royal standout]**. Everything seemed to go his way.

But then the strength and success went to his head. Arrogant and proud, he fell. One day, contemptuous of God, he walked into The Temple of God like he owned it and took over, burning incense on the Incense Altar. The priest Azariah, backed up by eighty brave priests of God, tried to prevent him. They confronted Uzziah: "You must not, you cannot do this, Uzziah—only the Aaronite priests, especially consecrated for the work, are permitted to burn incense. Get out of God's Temple; you are **[a royal rogue,]** unfaithful and a disgrace!"

But Uzziah, censer in hand, was already in the middle of doing it and angrily rebuffed the priests **[a royal meltdown!]**. He lost his temper; angry words were exchanged—and then, even as they quarreled, a skin disease appeared on his forehead. As soon as they saw it, the chief priest Azariah and the other priests got him out of there as fast as they could. He hurried out—he knew that God then and there had given him the disease. Uzziah had his skin disease for the rest of his life and had to live in quarantine; he was not permitted to set foot in The Temple of God. His son Jotham, who managed the royal palace, took over the government of the country.

. . . When Uzziah died, they buried him with his ancestors in a field next to the royal cemetery. Uzziah's skin disease disqualified him from burial in the royal cemetery **[sigh . . . a royal bummer]**.

Extreme Makeover

Director's Commentary

NOW SHOWING: *Extreme Makeover*

FROM THE BIBLE: Job encounters God while undergoing intense suffering (Job 1:1-3, 18, 19; 2:7; 5:8, 17; 8:5, 6, 20; 11:14, 15; 16:11, 12; 34:5, 6, 10; 38:3, 4; 42:1, 2).

RATED PG–13 FOR: natural disasters, death, intense pain, and anguish

POV: Accept the things you cannot change; lean on God.

KEY VERSE: "Do not let your hearts be troubled. Trust in God; trust also in me" (John 14:1).

The Lesson	Time	What you'll do . . .	How you'll do it . . .	What you'll need . . .
Take 1: Preview	15 to 20 minutes	Start off your lesson by introducing the theme with a relational, creative activity.	Option 1: Students act out "Fifty Percent Club" drama and discuss it.	1 copy of the "Fifty Percent Club" (p. 111); group journal supplies, markers (*Optional:* prop box; video camera, bedspread and pillows, a family photo, a plush cat; movie snacks for your audience)
			Option 2: Students watch a DVD version of "Fifty Percent Club." Or, choose to do both.	*Dark and Disturbing Stories from the Bible DVD*, TV, DVD player; markers, group journal supplies
Take 2: Feature Presentation	15 to 20 minutes	Dive into the Bible story and explore it together.	Small group and large group discussion	Photocopies of **Outtakes** (p. 112); self-adhesive bandages, permanent markers *Optional:* Bibles
Take 3: Critics' Corner	15 to 20 minutes	Help your students grasp God's point of view and wrap things up with a fun team-building activity.	Discussion, game, and prayer	Group journal; **Outtakes** (p. 112); prepared self-stick notes

WHY IS THIS PG-13 STORY IN THE BIBLE?

Why does bad stuff happen to good people? This is perhaps the oldest existential question around. If nasty people suffer, we might secretly think they deserve it. But when decent, innocent people suffer, answers blow off into the wind. *What's fair about that?*, we think. *Does God care?* Theology types have worked out answers for thousands of years—answers that make sense within a theological system, answers that remind us that we suffer the effects of a sinful world. However, when the question affects our lives, the lives of people we care about, or the helpless, theological answers can be distinctly unsatisfying. God can seem to us like an enigma who seems silent in our worst moments.

This is the experience of Job, a wealthy man who loses his worldly riches, his ten children, and his own health in a rapid succession of catastrophes you wouldn't wish on your worst enemy. His friends gather to console him, but mostly they miss the boat. In the theology of their day, three of his friends insist that because God is not unjust, Job must have messed up big time to deserve this punishment. The problem is, Job hasn't done anything wrong. Not a thing! And, just to cut a deal, he's not about to fess up to something he didn't do. He's even ready to tell God to his face—if he could see God—that he hasn't done anything wrong. He wants answers! Job doesn't turn away from God because of his suffering; rather, he's anxious for an even more intimate encounter with the Almighty. Finally, a fourth friend, named Elihu, speaks to the prideful tone of Job's statement and encourages Job to listen to God, opening the door for what God himself has to say.

We fret about the "problem of suffering" far more than the biblical writers did. Even God does not explain how it works. Instead, he emphatically reminds Job who he is: Creator, Almighty, Sovereign. "Where were you when I was busy making the world?" he asks Job. Job gets the point. God can take Job's honest questions, but in the end, God is still *God* and he's not held accountable to our human sense of justice.

Connecting with Community
Log on to www.darkand disturbing.com to connect with other ministries:
- Check out a sample video of other students in action.
- Share with other leaders at the PG-13 forum about what's working in your ministry, what's not, or how you used *Dark and Disturbing* or *Shocking and Scandalous* this week.
- Or ask for input about other aspects of middle school ministry.

Job's story will remind middle schoolers that there's a third factor in the justice equation: Satan. Some things will happen in life that we can't control—they just will. But we can depend on God to be God through it all.

Take It to Your Students

Here are some key points for your students in this lesson:

- When your life is great, don't take things for granted.
- When things go wrong, perhaps unfairly so, God is close by (even when it seems like he's not).
- Remember that God is God, no matter what. ✘

Extreme Makeover: The Lesson

Take 1: Preview (15 to 20 minutes)

Setup: This activity will set up the day's Bible story in a relational way as students watch a young teen open up about her parents' divorce.

Set design: Create a relaxed atmosphere for *Preview*. Ask students to sit on the floor in a circle on pillows, seat cushions, or colorful mats. The drama will be performed in the middle. Popcorn or movie snacks will help set a movie mood.

Makeup and effects: For today's drama, consider having students select props and costumes from your one-size-fits-all prop box.

Props: Supplies for the journal option you've chosen, markers; 1 copy of the "Fifty Percent Club" script (p. 111) or the *Dark and Disturbing Stories from the Bible DVD* and a TV with DVD player; or choose to do both activities *Optional:* prop box; video camera, bedspread and pillows, a family photo, a plush cat; movie snacks for your audience

QUIET ON THE SET

To launch the lesson:

- Welcome everyone to the group. Use first names or preferred nicknames and introduce visitors. After your students have had some time to socialize, pull them in and have them get comfortable.

- Go over your Rules of Engagement, if needed. (See the Rules of Engagement suggestions on p. 6 for more information.)
- Review the journaling component you've chosen for your group. (See Create a Group Journal on p. 10 for more information.)

ACTION

Either have students perform the "Fifty Percent Club" skit, watch "Fifty Percent Club" on the *Dark and Disturbing Stories from the Bible DVD*, or choose to do both activities. If you choose to have students perform the skit live, give a female actor a copy of the script and have her prep by reading through the script a few times. She might also want to rummage through the prop box for items to enhance the performance. Option: If you have more than one young actress who would like to try the part, and time allows, have multiple performances.

> **Option:** If you want, make a video of your students' live performance. Play it back for the group, the group and parents, or maybe the entire church.

PLAY BACK

Use the discussion questions below to reflect on the "Fifty Percent Club" skit with your group. Don't edit your students' responses—allow them to discuss freely. Also, have a volunteer jot "Fifty Percent Club" and today's date in the group journal, then record the group's impressions. Give every student the opportunity to comment or to journal, even if it's just to initial in agreement with posted entries.

Roxanne is struggling with the breakup of her family.

Use these questions to get a discussion going:
- **How does Roxanne see her life changing?**
- **Can she fix the problem? Explain.**
- **As a friend, what would you say to Roxanne?**
- **How have you dealt with something difficult that was out of your control?**

Roxanne can't change her circumstances. She wishes she could have a sense of control instead of her life feeling so totally *out* of control. She wishes she could understand what doesn't make sense.

The leading man in today's presentation is a good man—a man of his word. Without warning, and with a guest appearance by a heavy hitter, our good man's life slides painfully sideways. All seems lost. But redemption awaits in *Extreme Makeover*, up next. ✖

Take 2: Feature Presentation   (15 to 20 minutes)

Setup: Your students will take a close look at the story of Job and discuss leaning on God in tough times.

Props: Photocopies of **Outtakes** (p. 112); self-adhesive bandages, permanent markers
   Optional: Bibles

QUIET ON THE SET

Pass out copies of **Outtakes**, one per student. Optional: Have students grab their own Bibles.

ACTION

Use the **Outtakes** handout to introduce and teach the Bible story. First, briefly introduce the **Cast** and make sure your students know who's who. Next, use **Movie Trailer** to briefly cover the highlights of the Bible background and story. Then, read the Bible story (Job 1:1-3, 18, 19; 2:7; 5:8, 17; 8:5, 6, 20; 11:14, 15; 16:11, 12; 34:5, 6, 10; 38:3, 4; 42:1, 2) out loud or have volunteers read the various roles outlined on **Outtakes**. If you prefer, ask students to read the passages aloud from their Bibles.

PLAY BACK

Divide your group into two or more small teams for discussion with an adult or older teen leader for each group. Assign half the teams to explore the motivations of Job's friends (Team Talk 1, below), while the other half looks at Job's perspective (Team Talk 2). Remind leaders to be ready to enhance discussion with insights from **Why Is This PG-13 Story in the Bible?** (p. 103).

Give each team a supply of stick-on bandages and permanent markers. As teams dig into the discussion questions, have students write key words on their bandages about the motivations they see in their story characters, then stick the words all over one volunteer on their team.

Job is in a pretty bad place. Let's investigate what he and his friends think about it.

Team Talk 1: Get into the heads of Job's friends.

- **What do the friends' comments show they think about Job and why he's in agony? Are they right?** *("He did something wrong. He deserved this as punishment.")*
- **What do the friends' comments show they think about God? Are they right?** *("God punishes wrongdoing. God causes suffering.")*
- **Do the friends say anything that helps you understand the real reason bad stuff happens? Explain.**
- **Are these friends you'd want to have around when you're suffering? Why or why not?** *(Sure; they keep it straight when they're talking. No, they seem like horrible friends.)*

Team Talk 2: Get into the head of Job.

- **Do you think Job finds his friends helpful, even a little bit? Explain.** *(He doesn't agree with their stance that he did something wrong.)*
- **How does Job feel about God?** *("God beat me up." He wants answers.)*
- **Job was willing to go face to face with God. What does that say about his relationship with God?** *(He was secure enough to show his most raw feelings.)*

> Look for an opportunity to acknowledge that questions about suffering are tough! Your students are at an age when they'll search for more than simplistic, pat answers. Be honest. Say that everyone wrestles with hard questions, even if answers don't come immediately. That's part of the faith journey.

- **Does Job change his tune after his encounter with God? Explain.** *(Job is humbled. He knows God does not owe him an explanation.)*

Bring the discussion teams back together. Briefly review results of discussions by having the bandaged students stand up front; read aloud what's written on the bandages.

Continue your discussion as a large group by asking questions like:

- **How did Job suffer?** *(Loss of children, land, cattle; a wife who turned on him; painful, oozing sores)*
- **What feelings do you think Job experienced? How would you feel if this happened to you?**
- **What do you think Job learned about suffering?** *(It happens whether we "deserve" it or not; we can still trust God when we suffer.)*

- **Why do you think this story about agonizing suffering is in the Bible?** *(This is a good opportunity to remind students of the Key Verse, "Do not let your hearts be troubled. Trust in God; trust also in me" [John 14:1].)*

Job kept his promises, loved his family, and loved God. Enter: catastrophe. His friends tried to make sense of his suffering. But suffering isn't always logical, and that's the question Job struggled with.

Use these questions for more large-group discussion:

- **What choices did Job have to make in this story?** *(Whether to accept the advice of his friends; whether to tell God how he really felt.)*
- **Can you think of anything that could have changed what happened with Job?**
- **Does Job's story have any connection with your life? Explain.**

God may permit those he loves to suffer and bring something good out of it. Sometimes we can take action to ease our own suffering or someone else's. Other times, we have to accept that we can't change things. But God is still God, just like he was for Job. We can lean on him. ✘

Take 3: Critics' Corner   (15 to 20 minutes)

Setup: Reinforce the points you want your students to take away from today's lesson.

Props: Group journal with entries from Take 1; **Outtakes** (p. 112); prepared self-stick notes (see **How to Play** on p. 110 for specifics)

QUIET ON THE SET

Grab the group journal and ask students to gather to review the "Fifty Percent Club" entries recorded during Take 1.

ACTION

Consider the POV

Discuss Roxanne's options. Ask the group:

- **How can Roxanne best negotiate the sudden change in her life?** *(Accept disappointments as a part of life; try and accept the things she cannot change; tell her* *parents she wants to be included in family decisions; pray for peace; be patient with herself; form realistic expectations; search out peers who share her experiences; be assured of God's love.)*

- **How is God present when we try to make it through tough situations that are out of our control?** *(We have his Word; we can pray to him; he gives a sense of peace to those who humble themselves before him.)*

Draw students' attention to the **POV** on the **Outtakes** handout and read it out loud together: *Accept the things you cannot change; lean on God.*

Understand God's Truth

Hit on all sides, Job is desperate to understand why he "deserves" such pain and suffering. Ultimately, displaying trust, Job comes to accept what God knows undeniably: God alone knows what's best. As our creator, God knows more than we do.

Ask the group:

- **What have we learned from today's story?** *(God allowed Satan to test Job by taking away his "good life." Job learned to trust God anyway.)*
- **God restored Job's good life. What does this action tells us?** *(God is not an evildoer. He is the creator and restorer.)*

God raised the bar on poor Job. We don't know why. God doesn't explain it. But we know that God loved Job. And in his heart of hearts, Job knew it too.

Teamwork

Tormented in every way a man can be, Job looked to his friends for encouragement. The fab four gave it their best shot and went on their way. *Good going guys!* We can do better. Let's aim to be the kind of friends who help each other trust in God, even through the tough times.

PLAY BACK

Wrap up the meeting with a team-building game to help students reflect on the difference encouragement makes. Then close in prayer.

The Audition

Needed: small self-stick notes (or cut index cards and tape) prepared in advance (see below)

Got students in your group who love to be the center of attention? Who crack jokes or cause distractions when you're trying to teach? Games like this one are great ways to engage those students—to let them have fun, ham things up, and get a laugh in an appropriate setting. So encourage lots of laughter and goofiness during the "performances" in this game!

Goal: Figure out your identity in the game and encourage other players.

How to Play:

Ahead of time, think of various types of contestants who appear on TV talent/amateur shows (examples: rapper, comedian, ballet dancer, ventriloquist, tumbler, acrobat, guitarist, dog trainer, clown, yodeler, fiddler, mime, opera singer, magician). Write each type of contestant on a self-stick note.

When you're ready to play, stick a word to the forehead of everyone in your group without letting the person see it.

Each person in your group will try to figure out his or her identity by walking around and asking yes or no questions of others in the group, like: *Do I like to sing or play an instrument? Do I need to go to school to be me? Am I good with animals?*

Verse-ality: *I'll trust my Maker no matter what.*

Students can ask only one question per person before moving on. When a player correctly guesses the identity written on his or her forehead note, he or she should put on a brief performance to the encouraging applause of his or her partner.

After the game, say: **We need the encouragement of others. Be the encourager for someone who needs it this week. Live out this motto: No friend left behind.**

Close with Prayer

Ask your group to look again at **Outtakes** and repeat today's **Key Verse:** "Do not let your hearts be troubled. Trust in God; trust also in me" (John 14:1). Then point out this week's *Verse-ality*: *I'll trust my Maker no matter what.* If time allows, jot the verse in the group journal and have everyone initial it.

Invite students to share prayer requests, especially about any tough situations, big or small, that they're going through. Emphasize that leaning on God can make the difference in getting through tough times. ✘

Fifty Percent Club

Characters:
ROXANNE: a middle school girl
Scene: ROXANNE sits cross-legged on her bed, recording her video diary while snuggling with her kitten.
Prop Suggestions: Select any props or costumes you want from the prop box. Also have a video camera, bedspread and pillows, a family photo, and a plush cat (or just pretend).

SCRIPT

ROXANNE:

(ROXANNE sits on her bed, hugging her kitten. She reaches for her video camera to begin recording her video diary.)

Hey guys—it's me, Roxanne! *(She picks up her kitten and sets it on her lap. Roxanne is still quite happy at this moment.)* **It's time to talk about . . . what's going on today! I give you the inside scoop and the latest and greatest.** *(pause)*

Well, right now I am here, sitting on my bed . . . talking to myself. Say hi, kitty. *(She has the kitten "wave hi" . . . then suddenly turns serious and, flatly:)* **My parents are getting a divorce.**

(Roxanne drifts into a more somber mood.)

There, I said it. . . . They said that they tried really hard to stay together. Counseling . . . whatever. But . . . my dad . . . he travels a lot. And whenever he comes home, it's like my parents are . . . different. It's hard to explain. *(pause)* **My mom . . . she promised that we could go away this weekend. You know, kind of like a girl bonding thing. I'm really looking forward to it. I really, really hope she doesn't cancel.**

Anyway *(a sigh)* **a lot of my friends at school are divorced.** *(suddenly laughing)* **I mean, their parents. They call themselves the** *(overly dramatic)* **"Fifty Percent Club" because . . . 50 percent of the families they know aren't together anymore. . . . So, I mean, I guess divorce isn't such a big deal.**

(smiling as she remembers something) **My friend Gerard . . . He says that now is the time to ask for stuff, you know, things I really want. He said, I could figure out something and just ask. Wow. I'll have to think about that one. That doesn't sound too bad.**

And my other friend, Desiree . . . I really like her. She said that . . . She said that I would have to choose who I wanted to live with—my mom or my dad. *(pause)* **Sometimes, I'm like, it's gonna be OK. And other times, I feel like it's my fault. I mean, me and my little brother . . . we get into it a lot. He's just so annoying. And I feel kind of guilty sometimes.**

(setting the cat down and grabbing the family photo from the nightstand, turning it around to look at it, then turning it toward her recorder) **I'm really afraid for my parents . . . and my family . . . If we still are a family.**

(getting more intense while now looking into the camera) **Why can't things go back to the way they were? I'll clean my room. I'll even empty the dishwasher without being asked. No talking back—ever!**

(Hearing her name called outside the door, she drops the photo, lowers her voice, and leans in closer to the camera.) **I wish I could just make this sad, mad, bad feeling go away. Pastor C.C. at church . . . He says that God is there for me. Do you think? I hope so.**

(From off-camera, Roxanne's name is called again.)

Gotta go . . . we'll talk soon.

(She closes the camera and sits, thinking to herself. It's obvious she is very sad. Roxanne heads out of the room.)

(Skit ends. Have your actress rejoin the group.)

Outttakes

CAST

Job: loves God, but suffers great loss
Eliphaz, Bildad, Zophar: older friends of Job
Elihu: a younger friend of Job

MOVIE TRAILER

- Job is a wealthy man. Satan thinks Job loves God only because he has a good life.
- God allows Satan to test Job by taking away his good life.
- Job's three friends insist he has done something to deserve his suffering. Job insists he has done nothing wrong.
- A fourth friend, Elihu, angrily reminds Job that God does not do evil.
- When Job gets a chance to talk to God, God reminds him who the powerful one is—and it's not Job. Job is humbled.
- God restores Job's good life.

Verse-atility: I'll trust my Maker no matter what.

POV: Accept those things you cannot change; lean on God.
Key Verse: "Do not let your hearts be troubled. Trust in God; trust also in me" (John 14:1).

EXTREME MAKEOVER

Job 1:1-3, 18, 19; 2:7; 5:8, 17; 8:5, 6, 20; 11:14, 15; 16:11, 12; 34:5, 6, 10; 38:3, 4; 42:1, 2 (The Message)
(We've added a few of our own comments in bold below.)

Job was a man who lived in Uz. He was honest inside and out, a man of his word, who was totally devoted to God and hated evil with a passion. He had seven sons and three daughters. He was also very wealthy—seven thousand head of sheep, three thousand camels, five hundred teams of oxen, five hundred donkeys, and a huge staff of servants—the most influential man in all the East!
   [Plot Notes: Satan asks God to let him test Job. God agrees. Satan takes away Job's wealth by killing all his animals. Then he turns to Job's ten children—taking them away as well—and then derails Job's health.]
   . . . Another messenger arrived and said, "Your children were having a party at the home of the oldest brother when a tornado swept in off the desert and struck the house. It collapsed on the young people and they died."
   . . . Satan left God and struck Job **[again. This time]** with terrible sores. Job had ulcers and scabs from head to foot.
   [Plot Notes: Job has some friends with theories about Job's miseries.]
   Eliphaz: "**[Friend, you messed up!]** If I were in your shoes, I'd go straight to God, I'd throw myself on the mercy of God. After all, he's famous for great and unexpected acts; there's no end to his surprises. . . . So, what a blessing when God steps in and corrects you! Mind you, don't despise the discipline of Almighty God!" . . .
   Bildad: "**[Friend, you messed up!]** Here's what you must do—and don't put it off any longer: Get down on your knees before God Almighty. If you're as innocent and upright as you say, it's not too late—he'll come running; he'll set everything right again, reestablish your fortunes. . . . There's no way that God will reject a good person, and there is no way he'll help a bad one." . . .
   Zophar: "**[Friend, you messed up bad!]** If you scrub your hands of sin and refuse to entertain evil in your home, you'll be able to face the world unashamed and keep a firm grip on life, guiltless and fearless." . . .
   Job: "**[I didn't mess up, guys.]** I was contentedly minding my business when God beat me up. He grabbed me by the neck and threw me around. He set me up as his target, then rounded up archers to shoot at me." . . .
   Elihu: "We've all heard Job say, 'I'm in the right, but God won't give me a fair trial. When I defend myself, I'm called a liar to my face. I've done nothing wrong, and I get punished anyway.' . . . You're veterans in dealing with these matters; certainly we're of one mind on this. It's impossible for God to do anything evil **[no myth]**; no way can the Mighty One do wrong." . . .
   God: "Pull yourself together, Job! Up on your feet! Stand tall! I have some questions for you, and I want some straight answers. Where were you when I created the earth? **[Wanna see my playbook?]** Tell me, since you know so much!" . . .
   Job: "I'm convinced: You can do anything and everything. Nothing and no one can upset your plans."

[Epilogue: God gave Job back all his wealth and a new family.]

9

Director's Commentary

NOW SHOWING: *Rule #1: You Belong with Me*

FROM THE BIBLE: Hosea pursues his unfaithful wife (Hosea 1:2-9; 3:1-3).

RATED PG-13 FOR: strong sexual references

POV: Love is God's greatest gift; treat it with TLC (tender loving care).

KEY VERSE: "And now these three remain: faith, hope and love. But the greatest of these is love" (1 Corinthians 13:13).

The Lesson	Time	What you'll do . . .	How you'll do it . . .	What you'll need . . .
Take 1: Preview	15 to 20 minutes	Start off your lesson by introducing the theme with a relational, creative activity.	Option 1: Students act out "Faithfully Yours?" role-plays and discuss them.	Group journal supplies, markers; 1 copy of "Faithfully Yours?" (pp. 123, 124), cut apart; prop box, movie snacks for your audience
			Option 2: Students watch a DVD version of "Faithfully Yours?" and discuss it. Or, choose to do both.	*Dark and Disturbing Stories from the Bible DVD*, TV, DVD player (*Optional:* movie snacks for your audience)
Take 2: Feature Presentation	15 to 20 minutes	Dive into the Bible story and explore it together.	Small group and large group discussion	Photocopies of **Outtakes** (p. 125); several children's jigsaw puzzles (35 to 50 pieces); markers *Optional:* Bibles
Take 3: Critics' Corner	15 to 20 minutes	Help your students grasp God's point of view and wrap things up with a fun team-building activity.	Discussion, game, and prayer	Group journal; **Outtakes** (p. 125); sand pails, buckets, or large containers, prepared water balloons (see p. 121); permanent broad-tip red marker; minute timer *Optional:* paper wads or shower scrubbies instead of water balloons

WHY IS THIS PG-13 STORY IN THE BIBLE?

A man whose life is dedicated to God's work marries a prostitute—now there's a romance novel, some might say. But this is exactly what happens to the Old Testament prophet Hosea . . . and it's all God's idea!

The book of Hosea is a judgment cry against Israel, the northern Jewish kingdom. (Israel had split into two kingdoms, Israel and Judah, soon after Solomon's death.) Hosea's message points to Assyria as the world power that will subdue Israel, and it happens just as he predicts. But it's not unrelenting judgment; the book of Hosea also gives us a living picture of God's great love for his people.

God asks Hosea to marry a prostitute and have a family with her. Then God names Hosea's children with prophetic names that don't paint a pretty picture—names like "No-Mercy" and "Nobody." Even when his wife, Gomer, has an affair and leaves, God sends Hosea to find her and bring her home again. Despite Israel's disloyalty to God by worshipping Canaanite gods, the Lord wants his people back. Yes, they will be judged; yes, they need to repent. But more than anything, God still *loves* his people. Just as Hosea pursues Gomer and loves her despite what she's done, God pursues Israel.

Of all the prophets whose writings we have in the Scriptures, Hosea is the only one from the northern kingdom; all the others came from Judah, the southern kingdom. From Hosea's account, we have a clear picture of the depth of sin and unfaithfulness in Israel. The people have turned away from the one true God who loves them. They have fallen into false religions and worshipped false gods. They even practice the fertility rituals and temple prostitution of Canaanite religion. God is not overlooking this by any means. The people face the consequences of the choices they've made when Assyria conquers their land.

In this story of the love Hosea has for his wandering wife, though, we have the assurance that judgment is not the end of the story. What God wants is restoration. He wants to put the pieces back together. He wants to see his people thrive again in the security of his love for them.

Connecting with Community

Log on to www.darkanddisturbing.com to connect with other ministries:

- Check out a sample video of other students in action.
- Share with other leaders at the PG-13 forum about what's working in your ministry, what's not, or how you used *Dark and Disturbing* or *Shocking and Scandalous* this week.
- Or ask for input about other aspects of middle school ministry.

This Bible story will help middle schoolers see that love—genuine love—is something to take care of, not throw away.

Take It to Your Students

Here are some key points to put in front of your students with this lesson:

- Love is serious business; God doesn't give up.
- By God's grace, we receive the gift of unconditional love.
- We give God's gift of love to others through our actions and choices.

Rule #1: You Belong with Me: The Lesson

Take 1: Preview   (15 to 20 minutes)

Setup: This activity will set up the day's Bible story in a relational way as students act out role-plays, then freeze in place while "understudies" perform alternate endings.

Set design: Create a relaxed atmosphere for today's role-plays. Ask students to sit on the floor in a circle on pillows, seat cushions, or colorful mats. The role-plays will be performed in the middle. Popcorn or movie snacks will help set a movie mood.

Makeup and effects: For today's role-plays, consider having students select props and costumes from your one-size-fits-all prop box.

Props: Supplies for the journal option you've chosen, markers; 1 copy of "Faithfully Yours?" (pp. 123, 124), cut apart; prop box
Or, show the *Dark and Disturbing Stories from the Bible DVD.*
Optional: movie snacks for your audience

QUIET ON THE SET

To launch the lesson:

- Welcome everyone to the group. Use first names or preferred nicknames and introduce visitors. After your students have had some time to socialize, pull them in and have them get comfortable.

- Go over your Rules of Engagement, if needed. (See the Rules of Engagement suggestions on p. 6 for more information.)
- Review the journaling component you've chosen for your group. (See Create a Group Journal on p. 10 for more information.)

There are nine "Faithfully Yours?" role-plays. If you have a small group and you don't use them all in this first round of acting, consider doing a second round with the remaining cards. Have pairs switch roles, with the understudies now serving as the lead actors.

Option: If you want, make a video of your students' live performance. Play it back for the group, the group and parents, or maybe the entire church.

ACTION

One option for this activity is to show the "Faithfully Yours?" skits on the *Dark and Disturbing Stories from the Bible DVD* before having your students act them out.

Or, you can go straight to your own performances, or show the DVD after your group performs, and then let your kids compare.

Have your students form pairs. Call up two pairs; have one pair draw a "Faithfully Yours?" role-play card. Give that pair just 30 seconds to gather any props from the prop box and get ready for their skit; then have them improvise a performance. When they freeze (based on the "Faithfully Yours?" instructions), have the other pair—the "understudies"—step in and take over, improvising an alternate ending. (If pairs draw a card that's a role-play for the opposite gender, you may want to let them draw a new one.)

Continue with this pattern until all the pairs have performed for the group. When everybody's done, applaud for the performers.

PLAY BACK

Spend time reflecting on the "Faithfully Yours?" role-plays with your group using the discussion questions below. Don't edit your students' responses— allow them to discuss freely. Tape the cut-apart portions of the handout to the group journal. Jot "Faithfully Yours?" and today's date at the top of the journal entry. Have a volunteer record the group's impressions and performance choices in the group journal. Give every student the opportunity to comment or to journal, even if it's just to write their initials in agreement with posted entries.

When others don't care enough to give us their best, it just doesn't feel right. Let's look at today's role-plays.

Use these questions to get the discussion going:
- Which role-play connected with you the most? Why?
- Have you experienced unfaithfulness from a friend? What did that feel like?
- Who do you love spending time with? Why?
- Would others describe you as a loyal friend? Why or why not?

Today's reel-to-reel gives new meaning to the words *tough love.* Love rejected makes for a painful plot. But our hero is on strict orders not to walk away; he must return and win his bride back. A shocking request in *Rule #1: You Belong with Me*, up next. ✗

Take 2: Feature Presentation   (15 to 20 minutes)

Setup: Your students will take a close look at the story of Hosea and discuss the depth of God's kind of love.

Props: Photocopies of **Outtakes** (p. 125); several children's jigsaw puzzles (35 to 50 pieces); markers

Optional: Bibles

QUIET ON THE SET

Pass out copies of **Outtakes**, one per student.

Optional: Have students grab their own Bibles.

ACTION

Use the **Outtakes** handout to introduce and teach the Bible story. First, briefly introduce the **Cast** and make sure your students know who's who. Next, use **Movie Trailer** to cover the highlights of the Bible background and story. Then read the Bible story (Hosea 1:2-9; 3:1-3) out loud from **Outtakes** or have a volunteer read it. If you prefer, ask students to read the passages aloud from their own Bibles.

PLAY BACK

Divide your group into two or more small teams for discussion with an adult or older teen leader for each group. If possible, plan to make the groups all guys or

If you don't have puzzles, create your own by cutting pieces of poster board into shapes that fit together. Or travel to a second-hand store, where you can find puzzles for very little money.

all girls. Assign the guys to get into Hosea's head (Guy Talk, below) and the girls to get into Gomer's head (Girl Talk). Remind leaders to enrich the discussion with insights from **Why Is This PG-13 Story in the Bible?** (p. 114).

Give each group a children's jigsaw puzzle and markers. Students can write key words from their discussion, or emoticons—or both—on the back of puzzle pieces and then put the puzzle together. Or put the puzzle together first, picture side down, then write on the plain side. Have students use the Guy Talk or Girl Talk questions to discuss the motivations they see in the story characters.

What was God thinking? That question no doubt puzzled Hosea when God told him to marry an unfaithful woman and have children. Let's find out how it played out.

Guy Talk: Get into the head of Hosea.

- **God tells Hosea to marry a "whore" (translation from The Message version)—a harsh term used for biblical women who had sold themselves for sex and money. What kind of chance would you give that marriage?** *(Very little. None at all. Maybe a chance if there is repentance.)*

- **If you read just the first part of the story, would you see anything to encourage Hosea? Explain.** *(He has three great kids, but God gives them strange names. No, his wife leaves; this is not exactly a happy family life. No; God seems harsh.)*

- **Would you have blamed Hosea if he didn't want to chase after an unfaithful wife? Explain.** *(Of course not. Yes, he would still be disobeying God's direction.)*

- **What do you think is going through Hosea's head at the end of the story?** *(He did what God asked and he's going to take care of his relationship with his wife. There's no way to know!)*

Girl Talk: Get into the head of Gomer.

- **Gomer is used to letting men use her. How do you think she might feel when Hosea wants to be her husband?** *(Such love is completely strange to her; she wouldn't know what to think. Completely unworthy.)*

- **How is the love Gomer gets from Hosea different from the love she gets from men in the world?** *(Other men have been using her; Hosea is committed to her. He does the work involved in having a real relationship.)*

- **How do Gomer's actions show that this difference was not easy for her to understand?** *(She has an affair and leaves, so she probably doesn't really get that Hosea is going to love her no matter what. Maybe she doesn't think she's worth loving.)*

- **What do you think Gomer learns about love from this experience?** *(It's a gift and it takes work. It's not always what it seems.)*

Bring the discussion teams back together. Briefly review results of discussions by reviewing what students wrote on the puzzle pieces.

Continue discussion as a large group by asking questions like:

- **How is this story a picture of the way God feels about his people?** *(They disappoint him, but he keeps on loving and wants them back.)*
- **How does this story influence what you think about love?** *(It's a gift, and it takes work.)*
- **Why do you think this story about love and betrayal is in the Bible?**

Just like your pieces fit together to create a picture, God used the circumstances of Hosea's life to help Hosea see the big picture of God's love. Even when we think we're unlovable, God will go to great lengths to bring us back to him. Let's look again at Hosea's choices to live out God's love.

Use these questions to prompt more large-group discussion:

- **What could Hosea have done differently that would have changed the story?** *(He could have refused to marry a prostitute. He could have refused to take her back after she left. He could have refused to give her the love God wanted him to give.)*
- **How does today's Key Verse, 1 Corinthians 13:13, connect to this story?** *(Love is the greatest gift.)*
- **From your own experience, what do you think makes love so valuable? Who has loved you in the way God loved his people, and in the way he wanted Hosea to love Gomer?**

Repeatedly, God's people turned their backs on him—so much so that God referred to their actions in an offensive and degrading way. Still, God fought to get the Israelites back. He loved them. ✘

Take 3: Critics' Corner   (15 to 20 minutes)

Setup: Reinforce the points you want your students to take away from today's lesson.
Props: Group journal with entries from Take 1; **Outtakes** (p. 125); children's sand pails (one for every two players), buckets or large containers, lots of filled and decorated water balloons for outdoor play (see **How to Play**, for

details); permanent broad-tip red marker; minute timer

Optional (for indoor play): paper wads or shower scrubbies instead of water balloons

QUIET ON THE SET

Grab the group journal and ask students to review their notes on the "Faithfully Yours?" role-plays.

ACTION

Consider the POV

Discuss the contrast between the unfaithfulness of God's people and God's faithful love. Ask the group:

- **The Bad News: Israel's unfaithfulness was compared to a person who's willing to betray intimacy (sex) for money. Ouch! Why do you think God used such a shocking theme to display this message?** *(It's a super-bold picture of God's unconditional love for sinners.)*

> What is true love? Have students read the 1 Corinthians 13 passage to guide their answer to this question.

- **How are we sometimes like Gomer when it comes to our relationship with God?** *(We're not always faithful. We wander away from him.)*
- **The Good News: Love is God's greatest gift; treat it with TLC. What is true love?**
- **God's love story continues with you and your generation of young people. On a scale from 1 (low) to 10 (high), how strongly do you believe this to be true? Explain.**
- **JFF (just for fun!): God sends you a love text. What does it say?** *(ILU or LYWAMH—I love you or love you with all my heart)*
- **JFF: If God's love was an ice cream flavor, what flavor would it be?**

Jot answers to the JFF questions in the group journal. Then draw students' attention to **Outtakes** and have them read the **POV** one more time: *Love is God's greatest gift; treat it with TLC (tender loving care).* Finally, look again over the "Faithfully Yours?" comments in the group journal. Circle the one that best reflects today's **POV**.

Understand God's Truth

God's love is perfect. It doesn't break hearts. It neither abandons nor falls short. Treat God's love with the loving care it deserves. It's compassionate, loyal, and tender. It's his greatest gift to the world—and to you.

Ask the group:

- **What have we learned from today's story?** *(Hosea's life gives us a picture of God's great love for his people. We can love others even when our love is not returned.)*
- **Fill in the blank: True love is never, ever, this:** _____. *(Selfish, unfaithful, rude, jealous, and so on)*

In your relationships and in unconditional love for others, allow God to stir in your heart the true meaning of his love and faithfulness.

Teamwork

I'm lovin' it! **Faithful friends demonstrate true care and concern. With that kind of love, we feel valued. Be part of a team that lives this remarkable and unconditional pledge.**

PLAY BACK

Wrap up the meeting with a team-building activity that helps students reflect on the idea that love is a precious resource. Close your time together with prayer.

Love–Stuff Challenge

Needed: children's sand pails (one for every two players), buckets or large containers, lots of prepared water balloons (see below) for outdoor play; or, paper wads or shower scrubbies for indoor play; permanent broad-tip red marker; minute timer

Goal: Catch water balloons in pails perched on heads.

How to Play:

In this game, students will stuff their water pails with "love." Before the game, draw a red heart on each water balloon. Place them all in a bucket or container.

To begin, pair up throwers with catchers. (For large groups, form teams of two or three throwers for every catcher.) If you're playing outdoors with water balloons, have throwers and catchers stand at least 18 feet apart. (Use a shorter distance for indoor play with paper wads or the shower scrubbies.) Have catchers place pails on their heads, holding them open end up with their hands.

Start play: throwers gently toss one water balloon at a time toward the catcher, who tries to catch the balloons in his or her pail. (Balloons will break and players *will* get soaked!) After a minute or two of play, the team whose pail

Option: Divide into small groups. Have a volunteer come forward and then turn around to face his or her group. Place a pail behind the volunteer (about 3 feet), but not *directly* behind him or her. The volunteer will toss a water balloon or paper wad over a shoulder, aiming for the pail. This is difficult because the player cannot see the pail! The group helps, however, by shouting out directional tips. The pail with the most water or paper wins.

Verse-atility: *God's love is the best . . . greater than the rest!*

holds the most water wins the "love-stuff challenge."

Switch positions and continue play.

After the game, say: **Love is a precious resource. Don't waste a drop! Think of it as top-quality TLC from the creator of love—and meant just for you.**

Close with Prayer

Ask your group to look at **Outtakes** again and repeat today's **Key Verse:** "And now these three remain: faith, hope and love. But the greatest of these is love" (1 Corinthians 13:13). Then point out the *Verse-atility: God's love is the best . . . greater than the rest!* If time permits, jot the verse in the group journal and have everyone initial it.

Wrap up by inviting students to share prayer requests. Then pray together as a group. ✗

Faithfully Yours?

DIRECTIONS:

For today's role-plays, choose understudies for all performers. Have your actors in solo, pairs, or trios, as needed, for the role-plays below. Actors will perform the "unfaithfully yours" role-plays as written, then freeze in place, while their understudies perform a "faithfully yours!" option. (Note: the corresponding *Dark and Disturbing Stories from the Bible DVD* segment—"Faithfully Yours?"— has two such skits, which you can view as examples.)

✂ -

LOVELAND

Role-play: The dance is three weeks away. The seventh and eighth graders get invites before they run out. The sixth graders get none. The social committee shrugs off the shortfall . . . freeze!
Or the understudies do this instead!

✂ -

BABYSITTER'S CLUB

Role-play: Katherine is excited about her first baby-sitting job. Hungry, she goes for the kitchen to whip up a plate of nachos, leaving the children out front . . . freeze!
Or the understudy does this instead!

✂ -

HOME REMEDY

Role-play: It's late and Jake has a ton of homework to do. His mom's already asleep. He snoops in her medicine cabinet looking for something that will help him stay awake . . . freeze!
Or the understudy does this instead!

✂ -

THE LAST WORD

Role-play: Grace has a paper due on a little-known Civil War hero. With her friend's help, she finds a paper online with all the essential facts that she needs. Happily, she cuts and pastes the work as though it were her own . . . freeze!
Or the understudy does this instead!

✂ -

LUNCH BREAK

Role-play: Toby promised to meet friend CJ in the cafeteria. When he gets there, Nate invites Toby to sit with him instead. Toby says "Sure" and shrugs off CJ, even though this is sure to hurt CJ's feelings . . . freeze!
Or the understudies do this instead!

STRIKING BACK AT THE EMPIRE

Role-play: Auditions for the after-school choir program have attracted girls from a well-known clique. The choir director encourages Dion, who has a great tenor voice, to sign up. Dion loves to sing but doesn't want to be picked on by the girls. He decides to head home after school . . . freeze!
Or the understudies do this instead!

CHECKING OUT

Role-play: Shaun promised to check out a book from the library so Jace could use it for a book report—but he totally spaced it. When Jace meets him at their locker, Shaun makes up a story for why he doesn't have the book . . . freeze!
Or the understudies do this instead!

FEEDING FRENZY

Role-play: Jake gets Matt to feed his tropical fish while he's on vacation. The fish get fed Monday. Matt kicks back Tuesday through Friday . . . freeze!
Or the understudies do this instead!

FOOD CHANNEL

Role-play: The Sunday school party is in the afternoon. Zoey and Jim run short of cake mix the morning of the party. They head to church with half the cupcakes they need . . . freeze!
Or the understudies do this instead!

Outtakes

CAST

Hosea: God's prophet
Gomer: Hosea's unfaithful wife
Jezreel, No-Mercy, and Nobody: their children

MOVIE TRAILER

- God tells Hosea to marry a prostitute and have a family. Their marriage is a symbol of God's relationship with his people.
- Hosea and Gomer have several children together.
- The names of their children symbolize the crumbling relationship between God and his people.
- When Gomer leaves and has an affair, God tells Hosea to bring her back and love her.
- Hosea buys Gomer back, just the way God takes his people back to love them.

Verse-atility: God's love is the best . . . greater than the rest!

POV: Love is God's greatest gift; treat it with TLC (tender loving care).
Key Verse: "And now these three remain: faith, hope and love. But the greatest of these is love" (1 Corinthians 13:13).

RULE #1: YOU BELONG WITH ME

Hosea 1:2-9; 3:1-3 (The Message)
(We've added a few of our own comments in bold below.)

The first time God spoke to Hosea he said: "Find a whore and marry her. Make this whore the mother of your children. And here's why: This whole **[selfish and loveless]** country has become a whorehouse, unfaithful to me, God."

Hosea did it. He picked Gomer daughter of Diblaim. She got pregnant and gave him a son.

Then God told him: "Name him Jezreel **[an ancient battlefield]**. It won't be long now before I'll make the people of Israel pay for the massacre at Jezreel. I'm calling it quits on the kingdom of Israel. Payday is coming! I'm going to chop Israel's bows and arrows into kindling in the valley of Jezreel."

Gomer got pregnant again. This time she had a daughter. God told Hosea: "Name this one No-Mercy. I'm fed up with Israel. I've run out of mercy. There's no more forgiveness. Judah's another story. I'll continue having mercy on them. I'll save them. It will be their God who saves them, not their armaments and armies, not their horsepower and manpower."

After Gomer had weaned No-Mercy, she got pregnant yet again and had a son. God said: "Name him Nobody. You've become nobodies to me, and I, God, **[the creator supreme]** am a nobody to you" . . .

[TIME LAPSE. Notes: God gave Hosea's children names that represented his relationship with his special people, Israel. Hosea's wife cheated on him and left, just like Israel had cheated on God with gods that weren't true. Cut to a new scene . . .]

. . . Then God ordered me, "Start all over: Love your wife again, your wife who's in bed with her latest boyfriend, your cheating wife. **[For real . . . ?!]** Love her the way I, God, love the Israelite people, even as they flirt and party with every god that takes their fancy."

I did it. I paid good money to get her back. It cost me the price of a slave. Then I told her, "From now on you're living with me. **[Stand by me!]** No more whoring, no more sleeping around. You're living with me and I'm living with you."

NOW SHOWING: **Sin-bad**

FROM THE BIBLE: Ezekiel lies on his side for 430 days (Ezekiel 4:1-17).

RATED PG-13 FOR: one disturbing image after another

POV: Open your eyes and see the ugliness of sin.

KEY VERSE: "For our offenses are many in your sight, and our sins testify against us" (Isaiah 59:12).

The Lesson	Time	What you'll do . . .	How you'll do it . . .	What you'll need . . .
Take 1: Preview	15 to 20 minutes	Start off your lesson by introducing the theme with a relational, creative activity.	Option 1: Students play "Truth or Dare" and discuss right and wrong choices.	Group journal supplies, markers; 1 or more copies of "Truth or Dare" (pp. 136, 137), cut apart; 1 penny; Bibles (*Optional:* movie snacks for your audience)
			Option 2: Students watch a DVD version of "Truth or Dare" and discuss truth and situations in which it might be challenging to be truthful. Or, choose to do both—watch it and play it.	*Dark and Disturbing Stories from the Bible DVD*, TV and DVD player (*Optional:* movie snacks for your audience)
Take 2: Feature Presentation	15 to 20 minutes	Dive into the Bible story and explore it together.	Small group and large group discussion	Photocopies of **Outtakes** (p. 138); several pieces of poster board, markers *Optional:* Bibles
Take 3: Critics' Corner	15 to 20 minutes	Help your students grasp God's point of view and wrap things up with a fun team-building activity.	Discussion, game, and prayer	Bibles; group journal; **Outtakes** (p. 138) *Optional:* small- or medium-sized wall-mounted mirror

WHY IS THIS PG-13 STORY IN THE BIBLE?

There's symbolism, and then there's symbolism. In today's story, God asks the prophet Ezekiel to be a living symbol of a somber message.

Ezekiel lived in a time of political tidal waves. Assyria had demolished Israel, the northern nation of God's people. And now Babylon is smacking its lips for Assyria, and Egypt is on the prowl as well. Alliances shift like chess pieces. Babylon takes Judah, the southern nation of God's people, and totes off ten thousand captives from Jerusalem. Ezekiel is one of them. His ministry plays out in a foreign land to people who hope they can soon return to Jerusalem, their beloved city.

But Ezekiel's message is just the opposite. No, they're not going back to Jerusalem. No, Jerusalem will not survive the political tsunami. No, they shouldn't sit around hoping. The sin of the nation has brought them to this point.

Ancient writing at this time was done with a stylus in soft clay. For a permanent record, the clay could be baked. God tells Ezekiel to draw a sketch of Jerusalem in clay, build the signs of warfare around it, and lie there on his side as a reminder to all the people that their sin of unfaithfulness to God brought ugly consequences. Cow dung was commonly used as a baking fuel; God tells Ezekiel to bake his clay over human excrement instead. Ezekiel shirks in horror—he has never done something so unclean, so contrary to God's law. God relents and allows Ezekiel to use common cow dung, but the living symbol is powerful neverthe-less. Ezekiel's daily existence—for 430 days—cries out: "Don't sit around hoping for everything to be restored to its past glory in Jerusalem when you should be repenting."

A few years later, Jerusalem is burned and the temple destroyed. It isn't until the Persians crush the Babylonians five decades later that the Jews can seriously think of returning to Jerusalem—but to what? A capital in ruins. God is determined that the people will acknowledge him—even at the expense of his holy city. God allows Judah's corporate life to be smashed

Connecting with Community

Log on to www.darkand disturbing.com to connect with other ministries:

- Check out a sample video of other students in action.
- Share with other leaders at the PG-13 forum about what's working in your ministry, what's not, or how you used *Dark and Disturbing* or *Shocking and Scandalous* this week.
- Or ask for input about other aspects of middle school ministry.

down so he can renew his presence among his people and they will know he is Lord of the universe.

This story will help middle schoolers see that sin is nothing to gloss over. God takes it seriously, seeks our repentance—and offers redemption.

Take It to Your Students

Here are some key points to put in front of your students with this lesson:

- Denying sin doesn't remove its consequences.
- There's nothing pretty about sin, as tempting as it seems.
- Even when his actions seem harsh, God is looking after what's good for those he loves.

Sin-bad: The Lesson

Take 1: Preview   (15 to 20 minutes)

Setup: This activity will set up the day's Bible story in a relational way as students play "Truth or Dare" and share their views on acceptable and not-so-acceptable situations.

Set design: Create a relaxed atmosphere for today's game. Ask students to sit at a table or on the floor in a circle on pillows, seat cushions, or colorful mats.

Props: Supplies for the journal option you've chosen, markers; 1 or more copies of the "Truth or Dare" handout (pp. 136, 137), cut into slips and separated into piles; 1 penny

Or play the corresponding clip on the *Dark and Disturbing Stories from the Bible DVD*—or do both activities.

Optional: Bibles

QUIET ON THE SET

To launch the lesson:

- Welcome everyone to the group. Use first names or preferred nicknames and introduce visitors. After your students have had some time to socialize, pull them in and have them get comfortable.

• Go over your Rules of Engagement, if needed. (See the Rules of Engagement suggestions on p. 6 for more information.)
• Review the journaling component you've chosen for your group. (See Create a Group Journal on p. 10 for more information.)

ACTION

DVD Option: If you'd like, begin by showing your group "Truth or Dare" from the *Dark and Disturbing Stories from the Bible DVD* before students start this activity. It provides simple examples of how the game goes, which might put your students more at ease after they've seen other students do embarrassing things!

Option: If you've got a large group, you may want to divide students into smaller teams of five to ten participants for this activity. These smaller game circles will allow for more participation and add a sense of privacy and intimacy as students answer questions. Added bonus: it will help them get to know each other better and strengthen friendships!

Play "Truth or Dare" by selecting a student to come up and draw a card either from the "Truth" pile or the "Dare" pile. The Truth cards contain questions that the player must answer honestly in front of the group; the Dare cards direct players to do or perform something on the, well, daring level. Use as many cards as you have time for.

Option: If you want, make a video of your students playing this game. Play it back for the group, the group and parents, or maybe the entire church.

Have an older teen or adult take notes and record the "Truth" answers to questions in the group journal. Take notes on separate pages that can be attached to the journal. Jot "Truth or Dare" at the top of the entry and date it.

PLAY BACK

Have your group discuss their responses to the "Truth or Dare" game questions. There's a lot to discuss! Don't edit your students' responses—allow them to discuss freely. Give every student the opportunity to comment or to journal, even if it's just to place their initials with the posted entries.

Questions answered in truth give us a heads-up on the influence of personal choice in right and wrong decisions.

Use these key questions to get the discussion going:

Just a reminder that the **bold texts** in these lessons are suggestions for what you can say as you teach. Remember that this isn't a script; always feel free to take our ideas and put them in your own words.

- In your opinion, what makes a choice right or wrong? Who decides?
- If you wrote the dictionary, how would you define sin? (If you want, grab Bibles and look up Psalm 51:3, 4; Psalm 119:11; Isaiah 59:2-4; and 1 John 1:8-10 together.)
- Is sinful behavior a) something that just happens; b) a wrong choice or decision; c) no big deal; d) something everybody goes through; e) harmful to God or others? Explain your answer.
- Is wrong behavior ever the right way to go? Explain.

Speaking of truth, listen to this:

All butterflies have wings.

Airplanes have wings.

Therefore, airplanes are butterflies.

Huh? Something seems truthful and yet, at the same time, very false about this "logic," right? Sin is just as faulty and misleading. Once you recognize sin, it's easier to spot.

In today's presentation, the Lord of the universe is not in a happy mood. Fed up, he has his holy man become a living symbol of sin for his wicked-works-for-me people. It's a performance very few would choose willingly. *Sin-bad*, up next. ✖

Take 2: Feature Presentation   (15 to 20 minutes)

Setup: Your students will take a close look at the story of Ezekiel and discuss the truth about sin.

Props: Photocopies of **Outtakes** (p. 138); several pieces of poster board, markers

   Optional: Bibles

QUIET ON THE SET

Pass out copies of **Outtakes**, one per student.

Optional: Have students grab their own Bibles.

ACTION

Use the **Outtakes** handout to introduce and teach the Bible story. First, briefly introduce the **Cast** and make sure your students know who's who. Next, use **Movie Trailer** to cover the highlights of the Bible background and story. Then read the Bible story (Ezekiel 4:1-17) out loud from **Outtakes** or have a volunteer read it. If you prefer, ask students to read the passage aloud from their Bibles.

PLAY BACK

Divide your group into two or more small teams for discussion with an older teen or adult leader for each group. Assign about half the groups to explore God's perspective on what happens in the story (Team Talk 1, below) and the other groups to explore Ezekiel's perspective (Team Talk 2). Remind group leaders to enhance discussion with insights from **Why Is This PG-13 Story in the Bible?** (p. 127).

Place a poster board and markers on the floor in the center of each discussion team. Ask students to lie on their sides, with their arms within reach of the markers and poster board. Have students discuss the motivations they see in the story characters while lying on their sides. Emphasize that they may not change positions or move around except to use one arm to write. Ask them to write key phrases or draw pictures to express their answers to the discussion questions.

Can you imagine spending 430 days lying on your side? Let's take a look at why God asked Ezekiel to do such a crazy thing, and why Ezekiel did it.

Team Talk 1: Explore God's point of view.

• **What can we learn from this story about how God feels toward his people?** *(He's allowing punishment, but he still cares enough to keep communicating. He wants to show them he is still in charge, even after they've been captured. He wants to bring them back to him.)*

• **God is very specific in his instructions to Ezekiel. Why do you think this is?** *(So people will get the point that their ugly sin resulted in the consequence of losing their land.)*

• **God asks Ezekiel to lie on the ground for over a year. What's the point?** *(The people's sinfulness had been going on for years and years. Nothing was getting the attention of people; repentance was way past due.)*

• **What point would God make by asking Ezekiel to cook over human dung?** *(Sin is ugly! . . . It's come to this! . . . There's nothing pretty about it.)*

Team Talk 2: Get into the head of Ezekiel.

• **What's the gist of what Ezekiel is doing here?** *(He builds a model of what's happening. He's a living picture of what God is doing when he permits enemies to take Jerusalem.)*

- **Would you want Ezekiel's job as a prophet? Why or why not?** *(No way! Why not?; it sounds cool. . . . Are you kidding?)*
- **What does Ezekiel's response to God's instructions say about his relationship with God?** *(He obeys, except he doesn't want to be unclean with human waste. He's in tune with God. He can talk to God. He understands the ugliness of sin when he doesn't want to be unclean.)*
- **How would you sum up the main point Ezekiel is supposed to get across to the people?** *(Jerusalem is going to fall because of its ugly sin. Admit your part and turn back to God.)*

Bring the discussion teams back together. Briefly review results of discussions by looking together at the drawings or words students wrote on the poster boards.

Continue your discussion as a large group by asking questions like:

- **How does a visual aid help get God's point across?** *(A picture is worth a thousand words. It's pretty hard to ignore a living symbol.)*
- **What kind of picture of sin do we get from this story?** *(Gross; ugly; it has severe consequences.)*
- **Why do you think this story is in the Bible?** *(This is a good opportunity to remind students of the Key Verse: "For our offenses are many in your sight, and our sins testify against us" [Isaiah 59:12].)*

God asked Ezekiel to be a living picture to make a point: sin has consequences, and they are ugly ones. God wants his people back—even if punishment is the way to do it.

Use these questions to kick-start more large-group discussion:

- **Identify the key choices Ezekiel made in this story.** *(He chose to obey, but he chose not to pollute his own sense of righteousness with human dung.)*
- **What choices is Ezekiel calling other people to make?**
- **What does it mean that our sins "testify against us"?**

Ezekiel, in his awkward pose, was impossible to ignore. God wanted his people to get it—*really* get it. He wanted to open their eyes to see sin for what it was. Sin hasn't changed in all these thousands of years. It's still hard to look at, and we still need to recognize that. ✘

Take 3: Critics' Corner (15 to 20 minutes)

Setup: Reinforce the points you want your students to take away from today's lesson.
Set design: If you'd like, hang a mirror on the wall in your meeting space.
Props: Bibles; group journal with entries from Take 1; **Outtakes** (p. 138)
   Optional: small- or medium-sized wall-mounted mirror

QUIET ON THE SET

Grab the group journal and ask students to gather to review the "Truth or Dare" entries recorded in the group journal during Take 1.

ACTION

Consider the POV

Discuss the impact that sin has on our relationship with God. Ask the group:

• **Earlier we tried to define sin. How would you change your answer after our discussions?** *(Sin is a thought or behavior that falls short of the standards God sets.)*

• **Who determines what's sinful?** *(God.)* (Note: This may seem like an obvious answer, but it's a good time to remind students that God is the one who sets the standard, not friends and certainly not the media or our entertainment culture.)

• **What kinds of things result from sinful behavior? Give me some examples you've observed in your life, in friends' lives, or in our culture.** *(Broken hearts; damaged relationships; trouble with parents and with the law; separation from God)*

Ask students to open their Bibles to Exodus 20:1-17 and read God's Ten Commandments out loud. Have the group come up with two- or three-word summaries of each commandment and jot all ten in the group journal. Then ask the group:

• **What do these rules tell you about the relationship God wants to have with you?** *(Focus on God, not sin; think about his values and what he values in relationships.)*

• **How do we come to experience God's grace?** *(We don't earn or deserve God's grace, but he lovingly gives it.)*

• **How can we do better at living our lives God's way?** *(Live in the Word; obey my parents; keep healthy friendships; avoid sinful situations.)*

Draw students' attention to the **POV** on the **Outtakes** page and read it out loud together: *Open your eyes and see the ugliness of sin.*

Understand God's Truth

Exposed! God takes sin seriously. Sinful behavior is more than having a bad day. It's a willful attitude that's contrary to what God asks of us.

Inspire students in their effort to live God's way by reading Hebrews 12:1, 2 together.

Ask the group:

• **What have we learned from today's story?** *(Sin is a serious offense; God wants respect and acknowledgment.)*

• **Culture shock: Can God change people who seem unchangeable? Who bully, spread hurtful gossip, inflict pain on others, or cross the line with drinking, sex, or drugs? Explain.** *(Absolutely!)* **(Read Romans 12:2—pray for renewal and transformation.)**

It's easy to feel overwhelmed by sin. But we don't lose heart or hope! We can keep focused on God's constant presence with us. We lean on him when we are tempted or when we need forgiveness. Surrendering to his wisdom, we can live a life of potential and possibility.

Teamwork

Like an epidemic, sin is ugly and hurtful. When we let sin rule our lives, we send the wrong message. We're here to break that mold with God's grace and say that sin is *not* OK. As Christians, we share a life passion to be a positive influence in the community. Let's support each other in courageously taking a stand against sin.

PLAY BACK

Wrap up the meeting with a team-building activity that helps students reflect on rules as being good gifts from God. Then close in prayer.

Teen Lineup

Needed: no supplies needed
Goal: Cooperate as a team and line up in order.

How to Play:

Have your group scatter around the room and then state the challenge: **On cue, everyone must come together and line up side-by-side in birth date**

order—month, day, year, youngest to oldest.
There is one rule—no talking, no whispering!

Players must find a way to communicate
without *any* vocalization. Set a time limit
of 10 minutes to complete the challenge.
Communication may include lip reading,
ghost writing on backs or palms, claps, taps,
and stomps to count off days or months.

When the group is done (or time's up),
double check for accuracy by having students declare their birthdays out loud.
Congratulate the group on their great effort (even if they didn't get it right).
After the game, say: **Following the rules is a *must* for winning. God's rules are
rooted in real life and they exist to guide us so that we know what to do when we
don't know what to do! We have to play by God's lifestyle guide for joy-filled living.**

> **Option:** You can totally up the challenge-level of this game by adding a "closed eyes" rule to the no talking rule. Have students line up by day-of-birth only (1 to 31). Duplicates are possible, so they should line up side-by-side. See how your group does in 15 minutes!

Close with Prayer

Ask your group to look again at **Outtakes** and
repeat today's **Key Verse:** "For our offenses
are many in your sight, and our sins testify
against us" (Isaiah 59:12). Then point out this
week's *Verse-atility* (a personalized rewording
of today's verse): *My sins are evidence of a
broken heart.*

**Love's comeback! God's justice is under-
standing and mercy. He demonstrates his
love for us while we're still sinners.** Ask
your group to grab their Bibles and open
to Romans 5:8 and read it aloud: **"But God
demonstrates his own love for us in this:
While we were still sinners, Christ died for
us."** If time permits, jot both Isaiah 59:12 and
Romans 5:8 in the group journal and have everyone initial the entry.

> **Option:** Before students leave, invite them to come by your youth room sometime this week to pray on their own. Challenge them to stand in front of the mirror you've hung in the room, look at their reflection, and say to themselves, "Here stands a man (or woman) of God." Ask them to think and pray about what it means to live as a young man or woman of God.

> **Verse-atility:** *My sins are evidence of a broken heart.*

Invite students to share prayer requests, especially those that connect with
the main ideas of the lesson. Pray for your group. Also, encourage them to
take some time on their own this week to reflect on their sinful behavior and
to open themselves to experience the mercy God offers. ✗

Truth or Dare

TRUTH

Have you ever told friends you were sick when you weren't? Why?

What is the most important thing one person can do for another?

Share a time when you were misjudged, misunderstood, or falsely accused. How did it make you feel?

You're marooned on a desert island. Who comes for you and why?

Name something you really should have done for someone else—but didn't.

What celebrity do you most admire? Why?

Have you ever been tempted to cheat on a test?

Is survival of the fittest an unspoken rule at your school? Do you agree with that philosophy?

Who's the most exceptional person you know? What makes him or her so exceptional?

Do you enjoy listening to gossip? Why?

If you had 24 hours left to live, what one wrong would you make right?

What will you look for in a spouse?

What is the most cowardly thing you've ever witnessed someone else do?

What would you say to teens who steal other people's things?

What is your biggest pet peeve with social Web sites?

Name two things you could do today that would make someone you love happy.

Give three reasons why teens should not take harmful drugs.

DARE

✂ ---

Push a penny around a table with your nose.

✂ ---

Dance the Twist (or, your version of it).

✂ ---

Give a shoulder rub to somebody in the room—using your elbows.

✂ ---

Dance like you have ants in your pants.

✂ ---

Do a celebrity impression.

✂ ---

Rest your head on the shoulder of the person to your right. Now snore, loudly.

✂ ---

Sing an original song about homework.

✂ ---

Talk nonstop to the person on your left for 90 seconds.

✂ ---

Perform a cheer for a school team.

✂ ---

Pick a partner and sing "This Little Light of Mine" together. (Or another children's song).

✂ ---

Do 25 push-ups.

✂ ---

Mime your life story.

✂ ---

Create a thunderstorm by using your own personal sound effects.

✂ ---

Tell a knock-knock joke.

✂ ---

Perform a 30-second YouTube video about how to feed a pet tarantula.

✂ ---

Pretend to be a happy puppy. Don't stop until someone pats you on the head.

✂ ---

Recite the times table for the number 7 (up to 17 times).

✂ ---

Recite a nursery rhyme. (Make one up if you have to!)

Outtakes

CAST

Ezekiel: God's messenger, a holy prophet to the people
God

MOVIE TRAILER

- Ezekiel is God's prophet, telling the people what God wants them to know.
- God gives Ezekiel an assignment to graphically show (not just tell) the people what sin does.
- God wants Ezekiel to build a model of the military attack God's people will face.
- Ezekiel is supposed to lie on his left side for 390 days and then on his right for forty days.
- Lying on his side and looking at the model shows that God is punishing the people for their sin by allowing the Babylonians to capture them and destroy Jerusalem.
- During this time, Ezekiel will eat food cooked over dung. The people will suffer hunger.

Verse-atility: My sins are evidence of a broken heart.

POV: Open your eyes and see the ugliness of sin.
Key Verse: "For our offenses are many in your sight, and our sins testify against us" (Isaiah 59:12).

SIN-BAD Ezekiel 4:1-17 *(The Message) (We've added a few of our own comments in **bold** below.)*

[God:] "Now, son of man, take a brick and place it before you. Draw a picture of the city Jerusalem on it. Then make a model of a military siege against the brick: Build siege walls, construct a ramp, set up army camps, lay in battering rams around it. Then get an iron skillet and place it upright between you and the city—an iron wall. Face the model: The city shall be under siege and you shall be the besieger. This is a sign **[can't miss, like a flashing neon light]** to the family of Israel.

"Next lie on your left side and place the sin of the family of Israel on yourself. You will bear their sin for as many days as you lie on your side. The number of days you bear their sin **[brace yourself]** will match the number of years of their sin, namely, 390. For 390 days you will bear the sin of the family of Israel.

"Then, after you have done this, turn over and lie down on your right side and bear the sin of the family of Judah **[Israel's cousins to the south]**. Your assignment this time is to lie there for forty days, a day for each year of their sin. Look straight at the siege of Jerusalem. Roll up your sleeve, shake your bare arm, and preach against her.

"I will tie you up with ropes, tie you so you can't move or turn over until you have finished the days of the siege.

"Next I want you to take wheat and barley, beans and lentils, dried millet and spelt, and mix them in a bowl to make a flat bread. This is your food ration for the 390 days you lie on your side. Measure out about half a pound for each day and eat it on schedule. Also measure out your daily ration of about a pint of water and drink it on schedule. Eat the bread as you would a muffin. Bake the muffins out in the open where everyone can see you, using dried human dung **[Eew!!!!]** for fuel."

God said, "This is what the people of Israel are going to do: Among the pagan nations where I will drive them, they will eat foods that are strictly taboo to a holy people."

[Ezekiel now:] I said, "God, my Master! Never! I've never contaminated myself with food like that. Since my youth I've never eaten anything forbidden by law, nothing found dead or violated by wild animals. I've never taken a single bite of forbidden food." **[Mercy, *por favor!*]**

"All right," he said. "I'll let you bake your bread over cow dung instead of human dung."

Then he said to me, "Son of man, I'm going to cut off all food from Jerusalem. The people will live on starvation rations, worrying where the next meal's coming from, scrounging for the next drink of water. Famine conditions. People will look at one another, see nothing but skin and bones, and shake their heads. This is what sin **[an assault on truth]** does."

Cash Crazy

Director's Commentary

NOW SHOWING: *Cash Crazy*

FROM THE BIBLE: Judas betrays Jesus (Matthew 26:14-16, 47-50; 27:1-5).

RATED PG-13 FOR: physical attack, death, and suicide

POV: Getting what you want is not always worth the price.

KEY VERSE: "Do not those who plot evil go astray? But those who plan what is good find love and faithfulness" (Proverbs 14:22).

The Lesson	Time	What you'll do . . .	How you'll do it . . .	What you'll need . . .
Take 1: **Preview**	15 to 20 minutes	Start off your lesson by introducing the theme with a relational, creative activity.	Option 1: Students brainstorm "100 Things to Do Before You Turn 16!" and discuss their ideas.	Pencils or pens, photocopies of "100 Things to Do Before You Turn 16!" (pp. 149, 150), one per student; group journal supplies, markers; CD and CD player or MP3 player with upbeat music
			Option 2: Students watch a DVD version of "Truth Tell" and discuss their views on money. Or, choose to do both.	*Dark and Disturbing Stories from the Bible DVD*, TV and DVD player
Take 2: Feature Presentation	15 to 20 minutes	Dive into the Bible story and explore it together.	Small group and large group discussion	Photocopies of **Outtakes** (p. 151); lots of nickels, dimes, and quarters *Optional:* Bibles, paper, and pens
Take 3: Critics' Corner	15 to 20 minutes	Help your students grasp God's point of view and wrap things up with a fun team-building activity.	Discussion, game, and prayer	Group journal; **Outtakes** (p. 151); "100 Things to Do Before You Turn 16!" handouts (pp. 149, 150); basketball, tennis ball *Optional:* Bibles

WHY IS THIS PG-13 STORY IN THE BIBLE?

"How much?" We ask that question when we consider whether we want to buy a hot dog, a new flat screen, or a new car. Goods and services have value and individuals make the decisions whether something is "worth it."

So what is the price of betrayal? That is the question Judas asked.

In Jesus' time, day laborers received one denarius for a day's work. Judas, one of Jesus' closest associates, agreed to turn his back on Jesus for a price of thirty silver coins, which was equivalent to 120 denarii—four months work for the common person. How did Judas arrive at this price? How did he calculate the value of ending one of the most significant relationships he'd ever had? What was he trying to gain by walking away from what he said he believed? Was he really after the money? Or did he figure that if Jesus was going to die anyway, why not make a profit? We don't know what was in Judas's mind. For whatever reason, four months' pay seemed worth it.

We do know Judas was the treasurer of Jesus' group of disciples, so he was used to handling money and negotiating deals. Matthew tells us Judas went to the Jewish leaders to strike a bargain. It's possible they had already identified him as a weak link and approached him at a prior point in time, planting the seed in his mind.

At the last meal they have together, the other disciples are aghast when Jesus suggests any of them would do this. Doubt spirals around the table as one after the other wonders, *Who is he talking about?* Finally Judas leaves to do the deed. A few hours later, he kisses Jesus in a routine gesture of greeting and devotion to his teacher—but this kiss instead serves as a signal that sets in motion a long night of bogus legal machinations.

The next morning even Judas can hardly believe what he has done. In a panic of remorse, he tries to rewind, but there's no going back. Horrified at what he's done, Judas hangs himself (Matthew 27:5) and probably falls and splits his body open (Acts 1:18).

Connecting with Community

Log on to www.darkand disturbing.com to connect with other ministries:

- Check out a sample video of other students in action.
- Share with other leaders at the PG-13 forum about what's working in your ministry, what's not, or how you used *Dark and Disturbing* or *Shocking and Scandalous* this week.
- Or ask for input about other aspects of middle school ministry.

This story will help middle schoolers learn to think very hard when they reach for something they believe they want before considering the consequences.

Take It to Your Students

Here are some key points for your students in this lesson:

- Everything comes at a price. Is it worth it?
- What looks good at the moment is not the whole story.
- Some choices have consequences you cannot undo.

Cash Crazy: The Lesson

Take 1: Preview (15 to 20 minutes)

Setup: This activity will set up the day's Bible story in a relational way as students come up with ten or more fun activities they'd like to do, each for under $50.

Props: Pencils or pens, photocopies of the "100 Things to Do Before You Turn 16!" handout (pp. 149, 150), one per student; group journal supplies, markers; CD and CD player or MP3 player with upbeat music

Or play the corresponding "Truth Tell" clip on the *Dark and Disturbing Stories from the Bible DVD*—or do both activities.

QUIET ON THE SET

To launch the lesson:

- Welcome everyone to the group. Use first names or preferred nicknames and introduce visitors. After your students have had some time to socialize, pull them in and have them get comfortable.
- Go over your Rules of Engagement, if needed. (See the Rules of Engagement suggestions on p. 6 for more information.)
- Review the journaling method you've chosen for your group. (See Create a Group Journal on p. 10 for more information.)

ACTION

You'll be sixteen before you know it!

Pass out a pencil or pen and a copy of "100 Things to Do Before You Turn 16!" to each student. Read the "100 Things!" handout instructions out loud, then ask students to take some time to fill in their lists. Have everyone work quietly and on their own, but keep the tone upbeat with some background music.

As students reveal the ideas they've written, verbally affirm them. The more you intentionally try to create a safe and encouraging environment, the more likely they'll be to open up and share their ideas during fun activities (like this one) as well as during candid and personal discussions.

PLAY BACK

Ask the group to share some of the ideas they wrote on the handouts. Don't edit your students' responses—allow your kids to discuss freely. Have a volunteer write "Before We Turn 16" and today's date at the top of the journal entry, then record many of the activities mentioned. Give every student the opportunity to comment or to journal.

It takes brainpower to come up with a wish list—and on a budget!

Ask the group:

- Would having more money equal more fun? (It's OK to say yes if that is how you feel!) Why or why not?
- How did you do on your "100 Things" list? Options include: a) got stuck; b) no sweat; c) more money, please; D) I'm good!

DVD Option: You can launch into the next set of discussion questions by first showing your group the "Truth Tell" video segment from the *Dark and Disturbing Stories from the Bible DVD.*

Continue your discussion by asking:

- What things would you do with a boatload of money?
- What things would you do *for* a boatload of money?
- How about eating a bowlful of worms?
- What *wouldn't* you do?
- Would you ditch a friend for a price? Explain.

All that glitters is not gold—or silver—when a trust is betrayed.

In today's film, friendship has a price. With money in hand, the betrayer soon realizes his mistake. Anguish torments him, but the deed is already in play. And there's just no stopping it. *Cash Crazy*, up next.

Take 2: Feature Presentation   (15 to 20 minutes)

Setup: Your students will take a close look at the story of Judas's betrayal of Jesus and discuss the price of things they think they want.

Props: Photocopies of **Outtakes** (p. 151); lots of "silver coins" (nickels, dimes, and quarters)

Optional: Bibles, paper, and pens

QUIET ON THE SET

Pass out copies of **Outtakes**, one per student. *Optional:* Have students grab their own Bibles.

ACTION

Use the **Outtakes** handout to introduce and teach the Bible story. First, briefly introduce the **Cast** and make sure your students know who's who. Next, use **Movie Trailer** to cover the highlights of the Bible background and story. Then read the Bible story (Matthew 26:14-16, 47-50; 27:1-5) out loud from **Outtakes** or have volunteers read it. If you prefer, ask students to read the passages aloud from their Bibles.

PLAY BACK

Divide your group into two or more small teams for discussion with an older teen or adult leader for each group. Assign about half the teams to explore the motivations of Judas (Team Talk 1, below) and the other half to get into the heads of the religious leaders (Team Talk 2). Remind leaders to enhance discussion with insights from **Why Is This PG-13 Story in the Bible?** (p. 140).

Give each group a generous supply of "silver coins." Have students discuss the motivations they see in the story characters. Have discussion team leaders set a quarter down flat in the middle of the group, then dump the remaining coins on the ground around it where everyone can reach them. Each time someone makes a comment, he or she takes a coin from the ground and stacks it on top of the quarter. Groups can see how high their money pile gets

Just a reminder that we've included examples of possible student answers to some of the discussion questions in these lessons. You'll see them in *italics*. If your students get stuck on a question, share one of the sample answers to help them get their discussion started.

before it tumbles. If you want, also hand out paper and pens so someone in each discussion team can take written notes of the discussion.

Judas and the religious leaders are key players in this drama. Let's find out how seriously they took their roles.

Team Talk 1: Get into the head of Judas.

- Judas is one of Jesus' closest friends. What could make him want to betray Jesus? *(Apparently money; maybe he was having doubts about Jesus' teaching.)*
- Judas tries to act normal when he kisses Jesus. How does his attitude change after he sees what happens to Jesus? *(His conscience and sense of justice kick in. He can't be sorry enough fast enough.)*
- Step inside Judas's sandals for a moment: how do you think he felt at the key points in this story—when he got paid, when he points out Jesus in the garden, when he decides to end his life? What do you think was going through his head?
- Does Judas get what he wants? Explain. *(He gets the money, but he discovers the price is too high. He pays for his greed with his own life.)*
- What does Judas show us about the price of getting what we want? *(There are things in life that are not even close to worth it.)*

Option: To help students open up and talk more specifically about their own struggles with regret, betrayal, or money issues, create a more intimate setting by having everybody form pairs to talk about these discussion questions.

Team Talk 2: Get into the heads of the religious leaders.

- Jesus was Jewish and he was popular. So why would the Jewish religious leaders want to get rid of him? *(They didn't like his message. Jealousy: too many people are following him and not listening to them. They thought he was a blasphemer because he claimed to be the son of God.)*
- At what price do the leaders get what they want? *(Thirty pieces of silver; gross injustice; lying and working the system; destroying Judas along with Jesus)*
- How did the leaders react to Judas's regrets? *("Too bad. Not our problem.")*
- Why do you think they respond to him this way?

- **What does their reaction tell you about the price of getting what we want?** *(When we give in to greed and hate, we lose our sense of right and wrong.)*

Bring the discussion teams back together. Briefly review results of discussions by asking for volunteers from each group to summarize what they talked about. Remember to find out how high the coin towers got before falling down.

Continue your discussion as a large group by asking questions like:

- **In your opinion, what's the main thing Judas did not understand?** *(He might not have known exactly what was going to result from his betrayal. He might not have realized how he himself would feel.)*
- **Why do you think this story about betrayal is in the Bible?** *(This is a good opportunity to remind students of the Key Verse: "Do not those who plot evil go astray? But those who plan what is good find love and faithfulness" [Proverbs 14:22].)*

Judas *thinks* he knows what he's getting into. He doesn't. Jesus knows, of course, how God is going to use Judas's betrayal as part of his plan for Jesus to save the world. Judas, on the other hand, learns a bitter lesson: greed destroys lives.

Use these key questions to prompt more large-group discussion:

- **Point out the places in the story where Judas could have changed his choices.**
- **What can we learn about regrets from this story?**
- **What might Judas's story have to do with your life? Get specific.**

Let's face it: Judas loses sight of the big picture. And the Son of God will suffer because of it. And tragically, so will Judas. Being cash crazy is a trap any of us can fall into. Be careful with your choices. Getting what you want is not always worth the price. **✗**

Take 3: Critics' Corner (15 to 20 minutes)

Setup: Reinforce the points you want your students to take away from today's lesson.
Props: Group journal with entries from Take 1; **Outtakes** (p. 151); 1 tennis ball, 1 basketball
Optional: Bibles

QUIET ON THE SET

Grab the group journal and ask students to review the day's earlier handout entries.

ACTION

Consider the POV

Start the discussion with a simple physics experiment we call the "dead ball foul." Set a tennis ball (call it "regret") on top of a basketball (which is "a bad choice") and drop both to the ground at the same time. Amazingly, the larger ball will appear stuck once it reaches the floor while "regret," the smaller ball, bounces from the basketball and soars off wildly.

Judas made the choice to place Jesus at a disadvantage for personal gain. His self-important choice, however, fell fast and flat—like the basketball in our little experiment. On the other hand, regret, which may have started as a little twinge of guilt, skyrockets, overwhelming Judas and his will to live. Choices have consequences. And, sadly, regret is a big one.

Ask the group:

- Judas may have thought he really could use that money. How does what we think we need at the moment affect our choices?
- With today's story as a guide, what does today's POV *(Getting what you want is not always worth the price)* mean in your own words?
- What skills can steer young teens like yourselves away from becoming "cash crazy"? *(Identify appropriate and inappropriate feelings concerning money. Think of the consequences of putting the desire for money above relationships. See the difference between need and want.)*

Pause to write the ideas your students have mentioned in the group journal. Then continue the discussion:

- How can saving money, giving, and living on a budget help balance money's strong attraction? *(All are great exercises in self-control.)*

Look back over the "100 Things to Do Before You Turn 16!" handout. Did any of your choices include helping family, friends, or those in need? If not, think of a few now.

Allow a few minutes for students to add ideas to their handouts.

Understand God's Truth

Judas is a classic example of the saying: "Be careful what you wish for; you just might get it." Money can't fix the betrayal of a friend. Getting what you want is not always worth the price.

Ask:

- **What was the true price of Judas's betrayal?** *(Regret; a friend's death; suicide . . . No "compensation" was worth those things.)*
- **How can we keep regret in the background so we don't end up like Judas?** *(Think about choices, rather than rushing in. Have strong values. Stick to principles.) (If you wish, point students to today's Key Verse [Proverbs 14:22] and Luke 10:27 for discussion starters.)*

Judas has mixed loyalties. He is Jesus' friend and enemy. He's done the unthinkable in his dash for cash, and for what? Four months pay? Worst of all, he can't make it right after the consequences have taken hold.

Teamwork

You can call it "choice rejoice." Choice rejoice is making choices with God's values of faithfulness and love for your neighbor in mind. It's a great way to live and a great way to keep regret in the background. Let's be there for each other this week as we try hard to make choices God's way.

PLAY BACK

Wrap up the meeting with a team-building activity that helps middle schoolers remember a) to seek each other out to do good in the world they live in, and b) a good time with friends does not come with a price tag. Then close in prayer.

Body Workout

Needed: no supplies needed
Goal: Find a partner or partners to form an object.

How to Play:

Have players scatter around the room. Suddenly call out the number "two!" or "**three!**" as well as an **object** you want the pairs ("2s") or trios ("3s") to form as living sculptures. For example, you could call out "**Three—soaring eagle!**"

Students then rush to form trios and use their bodies to create their best version of an eagle in flight. Or **"Two—popcorn popper!"** In pairs, students need to create a human corn-popper. Fun objects you can call out include things like a panting dog, a laptop computer, a tree in a stormy wind, a

> If you've got a large group, you can also make four- and five-person living sculptures part of the game.

sizzling frying pan, and many more that you can think of! Christian symbols—church, cross, fish, lamb, dove, ark—also work. Challenge students to find *new* partners for every object you call out.

Applaud all pairs and trios for each living sculpture. End playing time on a unifying note by having the entire group come together with a shout of **"Everyone: runaway train!"** Let your students have a minute or two of fun with that one!

After the game, say: **We just worked together to make great living sculptures; we can also work together to help each other make great choices.**

Each day, the choice is yours. A wise choice in any situation is one that puts God front and center, keeps your conscience clear, and considers the needs of others.

Close with Prayer

> **Verse-atility:** *Plans for good find love that's faithful.*

Ask your group to look again at **Outtakes** and repeat today's **Key Verse:** "Do not those who plot evil go astray? But those who plan what is good find love and faithfulness" (Proverbs 14:22). Then point out this week's *Verse-atility: Plans for good find love that's faithful.* If time permits, jot the verse in the group journal and have everyone initial it.

Invite students to share prayer requests, especially those that connect with the main ideas of the lesson. Pray for students' requests and, more generally, ask God to help them make wise choices so they can live without regret. ✘

Directions:

One hundred is a long list . . . so, start small. Come up with at least ten fun things you'd love to do in the next two to four years, depending on your age. Dream big! Each entry should be true to God's Word, cost under $50 to perform, and actually be possible.

Examples:

Do a wilderness hike (week-long?/day?) with my dad/mom/family/youth group/class.

Create a winning burger recipe, then find a local sponsor to host a "Best Gourmet Burger Cook-Off" for 11- to 15-year-olds. (And win the grand prize, of course!)

1._____

_____

_____

2._____

_____

_____

3._____

_____

_____

4._____

_____

_____

5._____

_____

_____

6._____

_____

_____

7._____

_____

8._____

_____

_____

9._____

_____

_____

10._____

_____

_____

Extra Credit!

11._____

_____

_____

12._____

_____

_____

13._____

_____

_____

14._____

_____

_____

15._____

_____

_____

Outtakes

CAST

Judas: one of Jesus' disciples, who found himself facing a severe temptation
Religious leaders: Jewish leaders who did not like what Jesus said and did
Jesus

MOVIE TRAILER

- One of Jesus' friends, Judas, decides to arrange for Jesus to be arrested in exchange for money.
- When Jesus is praying in a garden on the night of the Passover meal, Judas shows up with a group of religious leaders and armed guards.
- Judas kisses Jesus. That's the signal that they have the right man. The guards move in to arrest Jesus.
- Jesus accepts what's happening as part of God's plan.
- Judas is full of regret—but it's too late.

Verse-atility: Plans for good find love that's faithful.

POV: Getting what you want is not always worth the price.
Key Verse: "Do not those who plot evil go astray? But those who plan what is good find love and faithfulness" (Proverbs 14:22).

CASH CRAZY Matthew 26:14-16, 47-50; 27:1-5 *(The Message)*
(We've added a few of our own comments in bold below.)

That is when one of the Twelve, the one named Judas Iscariot, went to the cabal **[plotters of secrets]** of high priests and said, "What will you give me if I hand him over to you?" They settled on thirty silver pieces. He began looking for just the right moment to hand him over.

[TIME LAPSE. Notes: At a special holiday dinner with his closest friends, Jesus says one of them will rat him out to people who want him dead. Later, when Jesus is praying in a garden, Judas shows up with armed guards.]

. . . Judas (the one from the Twelve) showed up, and with him a gang from the high priests and religious leaders brandishing swords and clubs **[tense, coiled, and ready to strike]**. The betrayer had worked out a sign with them: "The one I kiss, that's the one—seize him." He went straight to Jesus, greeted him, "How are you, Rabbi?" and kissed him.
Jesus said, "Friend, why this charade?" **[Heartbreak on the part of the Son of God.]**
Then they came on him—grabbed him and roughed him up.

[TIME LAPSE. Notes: Jesus was arrested and put through a false trial that same night. The religious leaders had to wait until dawn to get the final word that allowed them to put him to death.]

In the first light of dawn, all the high priests and religious leaders met and put the finishing touches on their plot to kill Jesus. Then they tied him up and paraded him to Pilate, the governor. **[Heartbreak and humiliation.]**
Judas, the one who betrayed him, realized that Jesus was doomed. Overcome with remorse, he gave back the thirty silver coins to the high priests, saying, "I've sinned. I've betrayed an innocent man."
They said, "What do we care? That's your problem!" **[Now get out of our faces.]**
Judas threw the silver coins into the Temple and left. Then he went out and hung himself.

Body Search

Director's Commentary

NOW SHOWING: **Body Search**

FROM THE BIBLE: Jesus handles Thomas's doubts (John 20:19-30).

RATED PG-13 FOR: graphic bodily injury; a bizarre request

POV: Express your doubts; Jesus is listening.

KEY VERSE: "Call to me and I will answer you and tell you great and unsearchable things you do not know" (Jeremiah 33:3).

The Lesson	Time	What you'll do . . .	How you'll do it . . .	What you'll need . . .
Take 1: Preview	15 to 20 minutes	Start off your lesson by introducing the theme with a relational, creative activity.	Option 1: Students act out "No Signal?" drama and discuss it.	Group journal supplies, markers; 2 photocopies of "No Signal?" (pp. 162, 163); some craft-making supplies like scissors, yarn, rope, etc. (*Optional:* prop box; movie snacks for your audience)
			Option 2: Students watch a DVD version of "No Signal?" Or, choose to do both.	*Dark and Disturbing Stories from the Bible DVD*, TV and DVD player; group journal supplies, markers (*Optional:* movie snacks for your audience)
Take 2: Feature Presentation	15 to 20 minutes	Dive into the Bible story and explore it together.	Small group and large group discussion	Photocopies of **Outtakes** (p. 164); prepared paper grocery sacks (see p. 156), scissors, pens or markers *Optional:* Bibles
Take 3: Critics' Corner	15 to 20 minutes	Help your students grasp God's point of view and wrap things up with a fun team-building activity.	Discussion, game, and prayer	Photocopies of **Outtakes** (p. 164); group journal supplies; 2 Hula-hoops, 24 balloons (12 of one color, 12 of another), several broad-tipped markers

WHY IS THIS PG-13 STORY IN THE BIBLE?

It's Sunday night, and it's been quite a weekend. Jesus' disciples have not exactly been at their best. On Thursday night, Judas betrayed Jesus (Judas would hang himself before even another twenty-four hours had gone by), and Peter impulsively chopped off an innocent servant's ear, then denied ever knowing Jesus. Three times. The whole group scattered from the scene instead of being there for Jesus. Among the men, only John was at the foot of the cross on Friday.

Even when the women came running on Sunday morning with angel-delivered news that Jesus had risen, Peter and John weren't sure they believed them and went running to look for themselves—and found an empty tomb. So now evening has come and the old gang gathers to sort through what's going on. But they're frightened. Jewish leaders may accuse Jesus' followers of having something to do with the disappearance of his body, so the group locks itself behind closed doors in fear and confusion.

And then suddenly Jesus is there, no doors involved. The disciples think they're seeing a ghost (Luke 24:37). Maybe they feel like guilty children who deserve a scolding because of the way they behaved on Thursday night and Friday. But Jesus doesn't even bring up what he suffered or what part the disciples might have had in it. His only concern is to calm them and prepare them for the days ahead by giving them the Holy Spirit.

So where's Thomas? He gets little attention from the other gospel writers, and only becomes important to John in the later chapters. We don't know where he is, but he's not there when Jesus appears and he doesn't believe what his friends tell him when Thomas finally wanders in with the group. We might wonder how many people would have to tell him the same story before he would believe. What did he think the others had to gain by conspiring to dupe him? He remains skeptical and is graphically specific that he will only believe if he gets to put his hands in Jesus' wounds—where his hands and feet had been nailed to the cross and where the spear had pierced his side.

> **Connecting with Community**
> Log on to www.darkand disturbing.com to connect with other ministries:
> - Check out a sample video of other students in action.
> - Share with other leaders at the PG-13 forum about what's working in your ministry, what's not, or how you used *Dark and Disturbing* or *Shocking and Scandalous* this week.
> - Or ask for input about other aspects of middle school ministry.

Another week passes. Once again Jesus appears and this time Thomas is there too. Jesus is not the least put off by Thomas's doubts. His attitude is "bring it." He offers to let Thomas do just what he said would make him believe—insert his hands directly in Jesus' open wounds.

This Bible story will assure middle schoolers that Jesus can handle their doubts; it's OK to wrestle through them.

Take It to Your Students

Here are some key points to put in front of your students with this lesson:

- Wrestling with doubt is a part of the life of faith.
- Take your doubts to Jesus; he's not afraid of them.
- When confusion leads to doubt, find your bearings in God. ✗

Body Search: The Lesson

Take 1: Preview   (15 to 20 minutes)

Setup: This activity will set up the day's Bible story in a relational way as students perform the "No Signal?" script, and then discuss faith and doubt.

Set design: Create a relaxed atmosphere for *Preview.* Ask students to sit on the floor in a circle on pillows, seat cushions, or colorful mats to watch students perform the skit, watch it on DVD, or both. The drama should be performed in the middle of the students if you act it out. Popcorn or movie snacks will help set a movie mood.

Makeup and effects: For today's drama, consider having students get costumes and props from your one-size-fits-all prop box.

Props: Group journal supplies, markers; 2 photocopies of "No Signal?" (p. 162, 163); some craft-making supplies like scissors, yarn, rope, etc.; or play the *Dark and Disturbing Stories from the Bible DVD*; or choose to do both activities *Optional:* prop box, movie snacks for your audience

QUIET ON THE SET

To launch the lesson:

- Welcome everyone to the group. Use first names or preferred nicknames and introduce visitors. After your students have had some time to socialize, pull them in and have them get comfortable.
- Go over your Rules of Engagement, if needed. (See the Rules of Engagement suggestions on p. 6 for more information.)
- Review the journaling component you've chosen for your group, if necessary. (See Create a Group Journal on p. 10 for more information.)

ACTION

Either have students perform the "No Signal?" skit, watch "No Signal?" on the *Dark and Disturbing Stories from the Bible DVD*, or do both. If you choose to have students perform the skit live, give copies of the script to the two actors and have them prep by reading through their parts a time or two.

> **Option:** If you want, make a video of your students performing this skit. Play it back for the group, the group and parents, or maybe the entire church.

PLAY BACK

Spend time reflecting on "No Signal?" with your group by using the questions below. Don't edit your students' responses—allow them to discuss freely. Have a volunteer write "No Signal?" and today's date in the group journal, then record the group's impressions. Give every student the opportunity to comment or to journal, even if it's just to initial in agreement with posted entries.

What does it mean to have faith? What counts?

Use these questions to get the discussion going:

- **What makes it hard for Jolene to reconnect with church?** *(She's been away, apparently for a long time. She may not be sure Jesus is real.)*
- **Would divine proof help? Why or why not?** *(Note: answers may be all over the board on this one, such as "sure"; "It would help me"; "No. We have the Bible and history, and if you're not going to believe that . . . ")*
- **Does having doubts make Jolene an unbeliever?**
- **Do you relate with Jolene's struggle? Explain.**

What's the secret to lasting faith? Faith-warriors tell us it's having persever-ance and patience, resilience and strength—in other words, hanging in there with God in times of great disappointment and doubt.

In a dimly lit room we'll meet the euphoric first responders to today's para-normal feature. A late entry, however, pits doubt against belief. It's an alternate reality of the divine kind in *Body Search*, up next. ✘

Take 2: Feature Presentation (15 to 20 minutes)

Setup: Your students will take a close look at the story of Thomas and discuss the relationship between faith and doubt.

Props: Photocopies of **Outtakes** (p. 164); paper grocery sacks (prepared in advance—see "Play Back" below), scissors, markers

  Optional: Bibles

QUIET ON THE SET

Pass out copies of **Outtakes**, one per student. *Optional:* Have students grab their own Bibles.

ACTION

Use **Outtakes** to introduce and teach the Bible story. First, briefly introduce the **Cast** and make sure your students know who's who. Next, use **Movie Trailer** to cover the highlights of the Bible background and story. Then read the Bible story (John 20:19-30) out loud from **Outtakes** or have a volunteer read it. If you prefer, ask students to read the passage aloud from their own Bibles.

Just a reminder that we've got some helpful insights about forming small groups in the Team Talk Small Groups section on pp. 10, 11.

PLAY BACK

Ahead of time, prepare for the Bible study time by cutting a small hole in the bottom platform of a paper grocery sack. The hole should be just big enough to put a hand through. Prepare one bag for each discussion team.

Divide your group into two or more small teams for discussion with an older teen or adult leader for each group. Assign about half the teams to explore Thomas's perspective on what happens in the story (Team Talk 1, below) and the remaining teams to explore the other disciples' perspective (Team Talk 2). Remind group leaders to enhance discussion with insights from **Why Is This PG-13 Story in the Bible?** (p. 153). Also, give each group a prepared paper grocery sack.

Thomas wanted to put his hands in the holes where Jesus' hands and feet were nailed to the cross and where a spear pierced his side. He was wrestling with what it meant to believe something he could not see. As we seek the truth in today's story, you'll put your hand through a hole in a bag and wrestle with writing when you can't see what you're doing. Do you have faith or doubt that you can do it?

Explain that as teams talk through the discussion questions, students should take turns putting a hand through the hole and writing on the inside of the bag. They can turn the bag to write on all the interior surfaces. Each student can try to write a few key words in response to one of the discussion questions.

There's some weird stuff going on in this story! What were these guys thinking? Let's find out.

Team Talk 1: Get into the head of Thomas.

- It's easy to get on Thomas's case for questioning what the others said. But are his doubts reasonable? If you were in his place and someone told you such an outrageous story, would you believe them? Why or why not?
- What do you make of what Thomas says it would take to erase his doubts?
- How does Thomas know that Jesus understands his doubts? *(Jesus offers to let him do just what Thomas said he needed to do to believe.)*
- What does Thomas's response (worshipping Jesus) tell us about faith and doubt? *(They can happen in the same person. Doubt can be fully overcome and replaced with faith and worship.)*
- Who is more afraid of doubts: Thomas or Jesus? Explain your answer. *(Jesus is not afraid of Thomas's doubts at all.)*

Team Talk 2: Get into the heads of the other disciples.

- The disciples are hiding in fear. Do you think any of them doubted that Jesus had come back from the dead? Explain.
- What do you think persuades the disciples that this is really Jesus? *(He shows his hands and side; he speaks; he breathes the Holy Spirit on them; they see with their own eyes.)*

- How does the presence of Jesus turn things around? *(They see with their own eyes; they are exuberant; they're ready to tell about what happened.)*
- Imagine you're one of the disciples trying to convince Thomas of what you've seen. What would you say to try to get him to believe?
- How do you think the other disciples were affected by Jesus' interaction with Thomas? What did it reveal to them about Jesus?

Bring the discussion teams back together. Briefly review results of discussions by carefully cutting each grocery sack open. (Cut along one seam and then along three edges of the rectangle bottom.) Open the bags flat and together review what's written (if it's legible!).

Continue your discussion as a large group by asking questions like:

- Why do you suppose Thomas wanted to be so sure about Jesus? *(Because he was so unsure! Because he knew it would change everything if it were true.)*
- Can doubts ever be a good thing? Explain. *(Yes, if they make us wrestle through to the truth.)*
- Based on this story, what would you say Jesus thinks about our doubts? *(He hears us even when we doubt; he's not afraid of the doubt of believers; he doesn't turn away from us because of doubt.)*

Thomas doesn't pretend to believe when he really doesn't. Without being offensive, he expresses his doubts. Jesus hears him and bears witness to his resurrection in astonishing supernatural form.

Use these questions to lead more large-group discussion:

- What choices did Thomas have about how to handle his doubts? *(He could have kept them to himself or even denied that he was doubting.)*
- How does today's Key Verse (Jeremiah 33:3) connect to what Thomas experienced? *(After we work through our doubts, God can give us even greater faith.)*

Thomas often gets a bad rap for having doubts. His nickname is, yes, Doubting Thomas. But because he expressed his doubts, millions of believers now see that Jesus walks beside them. Jesus is not taken aback or insulted by our questions. Express your doubts; Jesus is listening. ✗

Take 3: Critics' Corner (15 to 20 minutes)

Setup: Reinforce the points you want your students to take away from today's lesson.

Props: Group journal; **Outtakes** (p. 164); 2 or more Hula-hoops, 24 balloons (12 of one color, 12 of another), several broad-tipped markers

QUIET ON THE SET

Grab the group journal and ask students to review the day's earlier "No Signal?" skit.

ACTION

Consider the POV

Discuss the challenge in today's story and Key Verse. Ask the group:

- **How does Thomas challenge Jesus?** *("I doubt you're alive." "I need proof.")*
- **How does Jesus challenge Thomas?** *("I am alive." "Put your hand in my side.")*
- **Jeremiah 33:3 raises a challenge for us: "Call to me and I will answer you and tell you great and unsearchable things you do not know." How would you put the challenge in this verse into your own words?** *(God challenges us to get in touch with him, to seek him out, to call to him, to ask him things only he knows, to reveal his secrets—and he promises to answer.)*

Have the group work together to come up with a definition of *faith* that other preteens and young teenagers would relate to; jot it in the group journal.

Then draw students' attention to **Outtakes** and have them read the **POV** one more time: *Express your doubts; Jesus is listening.* Finally, look over the "No Signal?" comments in the group journal. As a group, decide on the one that best reflects today's POV and mark it with a star.

> If students need help coming up with a definition of *faith*, offer these starters:
> - Faith is a belief . . . *(in something you can't prove).*
> - Faith means being confident . . . *(that Jesus is real).*
> - Faith comes with a promise . . . *(of love and protection).*

Understand God's Truth

Without a doubt, questions are part of the faith experience. With today's true story you've been given proof, much like Thomas's experience, that Jesus can handle your concerns. Express your doubts; Jesus is listening.

Ask the group:

- **What have we learned from today's story?** *(Jesus offers to let Thomas do just what he said would allow him to believe—put his hands in his wounds.)*
- **What does Jesus' incredible, jaw-dropping, generous, and loving response to Thomas have to do with you?**

Thomas's doubt did not separate him from Jesus. Rather, it was a call to a higher faith. Jesus crossed the spiritual divide so that Thomas's doubts would be put to rest. Put your faith in God; let him help *you* put your doubts to rest.

Teamwork

Doubts are prickly, but they don't have to divide us. True feelings are something we can trust with one another in our group. Let's make this a safe place where we can ask our honest questions. We'll seek out the answers together.

PLAY BACK

Wrap up the meeting with a team-building activity that helps students reflect on the idea that doubt can be managed with wisdom. Close your time together with prayer.

The Ring

Needed: 2 Hula-hoops, 24 balloons (12 of one color, 12 of another), several broad-tipped markers

Goal: Secure as much "wisdom treasure" as possible.

How to Play:

The game is played like the Red Rover game most kids know. Divide your group into two teams by having each player count off as "1" or "2". Each team gets a Hula-hoop. Have teams place their Hula-hoops 30 feet apart, then fill their hoop with balloons. Use twelve balloons of one color for one team and another color for the other team's twelve balloons. With a broad-tipped marker, have students write today's **POV** ("Express your doubts; Jesus is listening") on balloons, one word per balloon. Make two balloon word-sets per team and place inside the hoops.

To play, have players join hands in front of their "wisdom treasure" of balloons. The game starts with a player from Team 1 calling over a player from Team 2. That player tries his or her best to break through the clasped hands of any two players on the opposing team. If successful, he scoops up as many balloons as he can hold on a count of five and rejoins his team—taking with him one person from the opposite team! If he fails to break through the line, he becomes part of the team that called him over.

Teams take turns calling players over. The winning team is the one with all the players and the most collected "words of wisdom."

After the game, say: **Give yourself a break and don't accept doubt's word as final. It's not. Talk to God about your feelings. Pour out your concerns. Get personal, as you would with a close friend. Shrink the gap of doubt between you and your Savior and discover that it's awesome to have faith—and an incredibly joyful thing.**

Close with Prayer

Ask your group to look at **Outtakes** again and repeat today's **Key Verse:** "Call to me and I will answer you and tell you great and unsearchable things you do not know" (Jeremiah 33:3). Then point out this week's *Verse-atility: Amaze me, God, with your wisdom.* If time allows, jot the verse in the group journal and have everyone initial it.

Invite students to share prayer requests, especially those that connect with the main ideas of the lesson. ✗

> **Game option:** Another fun team-builder goes like this: Place the Hula-hoop on the arm of a student and then ask the entire group to form a circle and grab hands. Without breaking hands, pass the Hula-hoop completely around the circle. *Can it be done?* Students will stoop, step, and wriggle to get in and through the hoop. For large groups, break into competing circles, supplying a hoop for each. Turn it into a race and see who can finish first.

> **Prayer option:** If you want, have students form pairs for your closing prayer time. Encourage them to share areas of doubt or spiritual questions with each other. Then have the students pray about them together. With this option it's best to have guys share and pray with guys, and girls with girls.

> **Verse-atility:** *Amaze me, God, with your wisdom.*

No Signal?

CHARACTERS:

SASHA and JOLENE: two middle school girls
Scene: SASHA and JOLENE are preparing decorations for younger kids, for an upcoming festival, by making various crafts. The crafts include foam cutouts, creations that use rope or string or yarn, and more.
Prop Suggestions: Select any props or costumes you want from the prop box. Also have craft-making supplies like scissors, yarn, rope, markers, etc., on hand.

SCRIPT

(SASHA and JOLENE are working in a children's classroom to help decorate for an upcoming festival. They're both deep into their work when light talk turns into a much deeper discussion . . .)

SASHA:
So tell me again why we're doing this?

JOLENE:
We're redecorating the room for the kids.

SASHA:
I know that . . .

JOLENE:
We're helping out Mrs. Kimsey for the family weekend.

SASHA:
Well, how'd you get . . . *(SASHA holds up the web-robe she is working on, to create a too-obvious pun.)* 'roped in'?

JOLENE:
She asked. . . . But I think she's trying to get me to come back to church again.

SASHA:
(They continue to work as they talk.) You've been gone awhile.

JOLENE:
I stay over at my dad's every other weekend. He doesn't live around here though.

SASHA:
What do you do instead?

JOLENE:
Instead of church? Well, I sleep in, get my nails done . . . and go shopping.

SASHA:
Of course. I think you should come . . . when you're here.

JOLENE:
Yeah . . . well . . . *(She continues, working in silence.)*

SASHA:
(being bold) **Church works for me. I've learned a lot. And I know this is going to sound lame, but I think of Jesus like I do my cell.**

JOLENE:
(a bit sarcastic) **You think of Jesus as your cell phone?!**

SASHA:
(looking up again from her work) **Jesus works through people. People I want to stay connected with. And whenever life gets messy and tangled up** (she holds up her web-rope again, but more seriously this time) **I call for help.**

JOLENE:
Like who?

SASHA:
Well, my mom, close friends. . . . And I could call you.

JOLENE:
I doubt that. (JOLENE holds her phone up to see if she has service in the room they're working in.) **Yep, no signal.** (JOLENE shuts her phone.) **Do you really believe that he's around? Jesus? Here with us?**

SASHA:
Yeah. I do believe that.

JOLENE:
A bolt of lightning would be cool proof.

SASHA:
A science experiment? Now that's lame. Jesus lives. His Spirit lives in me.

JOLENE:
OK, I'll think about it. (She returns to the coloring work she's been doing on her foam cutout.) **Hey! This looks great.** (JOLENE holds up her creation.)

SASHA:
I like it too!

JOLENE:
Maybe I should redecorate my room this color. Why should the little kids have all the fun?

SASHA:
And because you like to go shopping!

(Both girls smile.)

(Skit ends; actors join rest of group.)

Outtakes

CAST

Disciples: Jesus' closest friends
Jesus
Thomas: one disciple who was not with the others

MOVIE TRAILER

- On the day Jesus rises from the dead, his friends are afraid and confused, so they lock themselves in a room.
- Jesus shows up; he just appears like a ghost in the room. The disciples are thrilled.
- One disciple, Thomas, is not there when this happens.
- Thomas doesn't believe it when the others tell him what happened. He wants to put his hands in the wounds where Jesus was nailed to the cross and speared in the side.
- Jesus shows up again a week later. This time Thomas is there and can see the wounds for himself.
- Thomas's doubts are shattered, and he believes Jesus is back from the dead.

Verse-atility: Amaze me, God, with your wisdom.

POV: Express your doubts; Jesus is listening.
Key Verse: "Call to me and I will answer you and tell you great and unsearchable things you do not know" (Jeremiah 33:3).

BODY SEARCH

John 20:19-30 (The Message)
(We've added a few of our own comments in bold below.)

Later on that day, the disciples had gathered together, but, fearful of the Jews, had locked all the doors in the house. Jesus entered **[. . . how?]**, stood among them, and said, "Peace to you." Then he showed them his hands and side.

The disciples, seeing the Master with their own eyes, were exuberant. Jesus repeated his greeting: "Peace to you. Just as the Father sent me, I send you."

Then he took a deep breath and breathed into them. "Receive the Holy Spirit," he said. "If you forgive someone's sins, they're gone for good. If you don't forgive sins, what are you going to do with them?"

But Thomas, sometimes called the Twin, one of the Twelve, was not with them when Jesus came. The other disciples told him, "We saw the Master."

But he said, "Unless I see the nail holes in his hands, put my finger in the nail holes, and stick my hand in his side, I won't believe it." **[In other words: Prove it!]**

Eight days later, his disciples were again in the room. This time Thomas was with them. Jesus came through the locked doors **[there he goes again!]**, stood among them, and said, "Peace to you."

Then he focused his attention on Thomas. "Take your finger and examine my hands. Take your hand and stick it in my side. **[No joke!]** Don't be unbelieving. Believe."

Thomas said, "My Master! My God!"

Jesus said, "So, you believe because you've seen with your own eyes. Even better blessings are in store for those who believe without seeing." **[That's you and me.]**

Jesus provided far more God-revealing signs than are written down in this book. These are written down so you will believe that Jesus is the Messiah, the Son of God, and in the act of believing, have real and eternal life **[outstanding, remarkable, awesome life]** in the way he personally revealed it.

Director's Commentary

NOW SHOWING: *To Die For*

FROM THE BIBLE: Ananias and Sapphira lie to God (Acts 4:32; 5:1-10).

RATED PG-13 FOR: premeditated deceit and instantaneous death

POV: Lying to look good almost always backfires.

KEY VERSE: "I strive always to keep my conscience clear before God and man" (Acts 24:16).

The Lesson	Time	What you'll do . . .	How you'll do it . . .	What you'll need . . .
Take 1: Preview	15 to 20 minutes	Start off your lesson by introducing the theme with a relational, creative activity.	Option 1: Students participate in a hands-on object lesson, then work in pairs to create funny stories about lying.	1 can of mandarin oranges, 1 brown paper lunch bag (see p. 168); pencils, photocopies of "Gotcha!" (p. 175), 1 per pair of students; group journal supplies, markers (*Optional:* paper clips or stapler)
			Option 2: Students watch a DVD version of "Backfire Lies" and then discuss their owns views on lies and deceit. Or, choose to do both.	*Dark and Disturbing Stories from the Bible DVD*, TV and DVD player
Take 2: Feature Presentation	15 to 20 minutes	Dive into the Bible story and explore it together.	Small group and large group discussion	**Outtakes** (p. 176), 1 copy per student; envelopes, bank deposit slips or plain paper, markers *Optional:* Bibles, wallets
Take 3: Critics' Corner	15 to 20 minutes	Help your students grasp God's point of view and wrap things up with a fun team-building activity.	Discussion, game, and prayer	**Outtakes** (p. 176); group journal; 2 buckets, 1 beanbag, timer

WHY IS THIS PG-13 STORY IN THE BIBLE?

Even the earliest Christian church—the one chronologically closest to the life of Jesus—was not perfect. The Holy Spirit came at Pentecost, a feast time that filled Jerusalem's streets with thousands of extra people from around the Roman Empire. Many believed in Jesus and perhaps stayed in Jerusalem to grow in their faith. The needs of these long-term visitors may have been the impetus behind the believers' decision to share their personal belongings for the good of the growing church (Acts 4:32). But people are still people, and Satan is always still on the prowl.

In Acts 5, two Christians named Ananias and Sapphira sell a field and bring a generous offering to the church leaders. So far, so good. Their mistake is not in holding back part of the profit. The communal attitude toward possessions was voluntary, and it's completely reasonable that people should look after their own needs while also being generous toward the needs of others. Their mistake—their sin—is in telling Peter and the other apostles that they are donating every last cent. They lie to make themselves look good, plain and simple. They want recognition for the complete self-sacrifice of their gift. When they lie to Peter, they lie to God, and they hadn't reckoned on God letting Peter in on their deception. Each of them is responsible for the choice they made together, and they pay with their lives.

Connecting with Community

Log on to www.darkand disturbing.com to connect with other ministries:

- Check out a sample video of other students in action.
- Share with other leaders at the PG-13 forum about what's working in your ministry, what's not, or how you used *Dark and Disturbing* or *Shocking and Scandalous* this week.
- Or ask for input about other aspects of middle school ministry.

Being struck dead for what we might think is a forgivable offense under God's grace sounds Old Testament-ish. In fact, Leviticus 10 tells a similar story; God struck down the sons of Aaron because they flagrantly disrespected God. The Leviticus story lets Israel, God's people newly freed from slavery, know he sees their hearts. The Acts story lets God's people, the church, know they can't deceive him. Unchecked, the dishonesty, greed, and hidden motives of Ananias and Sapphira could have begun a destructive pattern at a crucial time in the life of the new church.

Christian life is not "every man for himself." We share a common life. What we do affects other people. No matter how much we may convince ourselves of the rightness of a choice—no matter how well we stick to that story—God knows the truth.

This Bible story will help middle school students understand that lying to make themselves look good is a destructive habit that God wants to shake them from.

Take It to Your Students

Here are some key points for your students in this lesson:

- Lying to look good actually produces the opposite result.
- Lying easily becomes a pattern, and it's a destructive habit at that.
- Honesty is a trait others hope to see in you. ✘

To Die For: The Lesson

Take 1: Preview   (15 to 20 minutes)

Setup: This activity will set up the day's Bible story in a relational way through a hands-on (and surprising!) object lesson followed by a fun challenge for pairs.

Props: 1 can of mandarin oranges, 1 brown paper lunch bag (prepped in advance—see below); pencils, photocopies of "Gotcha!" (p. 175), 1 per pair of students; group journal supplies, markers
(*Optional:* paper clips or stapler)
Or play the corresponding clip on the *Dark and Disturbing Stories from the Bible DVD* segment ("Backfire Lies")—or do both activities.

QUIET ON THE SET

To launch the lesson:

- Welcome everyone to the group. Use first names or preferred nicknames and introduce visitors. After your students have had some time to socialize, pull them in and have them get comfortable.
- Go over your Rules of Engagement, if needed. (See the Rules of Engagement suggestions on p. 6 for more information.)
- Review the journaling method you've chosen for your group. (See Create a Group Journal on p. 10 for more information.)

ACTION

Before your time with the students, open a can of mandarin oranges and drain thoroughly. Place the open can in a brown lunch bag and close up the bag. (*Caution:* If the can has rough or sharp edges that can cut, place the fruit in a cup instead, then put the cup in the bag.)

Tell the following tall-tale to your group: **Before our meeting I stopped and bought food for my** (son's/daughter's/friend's) **pet** (lizard/turtle/bird/fish). (Hold up the lunch bag you prepared.) **Live caterpillars are a special treat for Brutus. But these unusually large ones need special handling. Believe it or not they like to be petted. Who'd like the job?** (Pause for volunteers.) **Be careful. Cranky caterpillars bite.**

Students will be suspicious but intrigued. Have the brave ones reach into the lunch bag (no peeking allowed!) to pet the "caterpillars." Shake the bag once or twice to give your volunteers a start. After a time, reveal your little ruse and have students guess what's really in the bag. Open the bag to reveal your "wormy" orange slices. Say: **My tall tale got a few of you guys!**

Ask students to pair up, then distribute the "Gotcha!" handouts, one per pair. Have students fold the handout in half and then work together with their partner to fill in the words on the top half. When they're done, they can open the page up and plug in their words to read the story at the bottom.

PLAY BACK

Ask the pairs to share their inventive stories from the handouts. Have a volunteer jot "Gotcha!" and today's date at the top of the journal entry. Slip in, clip, or staple completed handouts to the group journal page. Also jot down impressions from the group discussion questions below.

Fun stories! No matter the story, though, your main character got cornered for trying to hide the truth.

Use these questions to launch discussion:

- How do you suppose the main character feels about lying at the end of the story?
- In your experience, what are the chances of getting caught in a lie? a) 100 percent; b) pretty good; c) 50/50; d) slim to none; e) it raises suspicions, so I don't go there.

DVD Option: Watch "Backfire Lies" from the *Dark and Disturbing Stories from the Bible DVD* and then have your students talk through some of the discussion questions below:

- When you were a little kid, were you ever caught in a lie? What did you lie about? How did your parents handle it?
- How about now that you're older: Ever had a lie backfire? Share what you experienced.
- Is the habit of lying easy to break? Why or why not?

Tricking people can be fun, but as we've discussed, lying often produces unexpected aftershocks.

In this week's feature, the world seems a perfect place until a lie ruptures the calm. God's objective is clear: root out the contamination before it has a chance to infect others. *To Die For,* up next. ✖

Take 2: Feature Presentation (15 to 20 minutes)

Setup: Your students will take a close look at the story of Ananias and Sapphira and discuss what really happens when we lie.

Props: Photocopies of **Outtakes** (p. 176); envelopes, bank deposit slips or plain paper, markers

Optional: Bibles, wallets

QUIET ON THE SET
Pass out copies of **Outtakes**, one per student. Optional: Have students grab their own Bibles.

ACTION
Use **Outtakes** with your students to introduce and teach the Bible story. First, briefly introduce the **Cast** and make sure your students know who's who. Next, use **Movie Trailer** to cover the highlights of the Bible background and story. Then read the Bible story (Acts 4:32; 5:1-10) out loud from **Outtakes** or have a volunteer read it. If you prefer, ask students to read the passages aloud from their own Bibles.

PLAY BACK
Divide your group into two or more small teams for discussion with an older teen or adult leader for each group. Assign about half of the teams to get into

the heads of Ananias and Sapphira (Team Talk 1, below) and the remaining teams to get into the heads of Peter and the other apostles (Team Talk 2). Remind leaders to enrich the discussion with insights from **Why Is This PG-13 Story in the Bible?** (p. 166).

Option: If you want, use wallets for the deposit slip activity instead of envelopes.

Give each group markers and an envelope filled with bank deposit slips (or slips of plain paper with dollar signs—$$$—on them). In front of everyone, take one slip out of one of the team's envelopes. Say: **I'm going to write a number on this slip to represent a bank balance.** Pause and write a number on a slip without anyone seeing what you wrote, then fold it and set it aside.

Tell students a number; explain that it may or may not be the one you wrote on the deposit slip. (You decide if you want to tell the truth or say a different number—the activity works either way.) Explain the rest of the activity to the group: As students discuss the questions, they pass their envelope around their team circle. Each student should take one slip and write "yes" if they think you told the truth about the bank balance or "no" if they think you didn't. Challenge them to also each write an answer to one of the discussion questions on their deposit slip. Once a student has written yes or no and an answer, he should pass the envelope to the next person.

In our story, Peter provides a safety net for Ananias and Sapphira. But the couple decides to pass and things unravel pretty quickly for them.

Team Talk 1: Get into the heads of Ananias and Sapphira.

- **Why would Ananias and Sapphira lie?** *(Satan's influence. They want to look good.)* **What do they hope to gain?** *(Recognition.)*
- **What do you think their thought process was? How do you think they justified their little "white lie" to themselves?**
- **What does their lie tell us they really think about the group's agreement to be generous?** *(They know being generous looks good, but they put limits on how much they want to actually sacrifice.)*
- **They plan their lie ahead of time. Does that make it worse than lying on the spot? Why or why not?** *(No—A lie is a lie. Yes—they purposefully want to be deceitful.)*
- **Imagine things turned our differently: suppose Sapphira knew what happened to her husband and she decided to answer differently. Would she still be guilty**

of lying? Why or why not? *(She was in on the original plan to lie. Her life might have been spared if she'd come clean, however; this would have shown repentance.)*

Team Talk 2: Get into the heads of Peter and the other apostles.

- **What might Peter and the others have thought if Ananias and Sapphira were honest about keeping some money?** *(There was no rule that they couldn't keep something.)*
- **Was it wrong for them to keep some? Why or why not?** *(Their sin was lying about it.)*
- **Imagine you were there when Ananias died. What would you have thought or felt or wondered? Explain.**
- **What happens to Ananias is a lesson to everyone watching. What does this tell us about the danger of lying?** *(Our words have power. God is always watching.)*
- **Peter could have told Sapphira what happened to her husband. So why doesn't he?** *(He gives her a chance to come clean and perhaps be spared.)*
- **Peter mentions the Holy Spirit to both Ananias and Sapphira. Why do you think he does this?** *(To make it clear that we can't fool God.)*

Bring the discussion teams back together. Briefly review results of discussions by reading some of the comments written on the deposit slips. Tally the "votes" to see if students thought you were truthful, then reveal the number you wrote down.

Continue discussion as a large group by asking questions like:

- **Is it possible to lie to God? Why or why not?** *(We can try, but we really can't. We're just fooling ourselves.)*
- **Ananias and Sapphira lied to make themselves look good. What about today—in your world? Name some common reasons people lie to make themselves look good.**
- **Why do you think this story about lying is in the Bible?**

Ananias and Sapphira thought that as long as they kept their secret, no one would get hurt. They had no idea what was in store for them when they chose to "impress" with their few-bucks-short offering.

Use these questions to continue with more large-group discussion:

- **Who gets hurt by a lie?** *(Other people; God; ourselves)*
- **What's the difference between secrets and lying? When does a secret turn into a lie?**

Review the **Key Verse** (Acts 24:16) together and then work together to brainstorm the advantages of having a clear conscience.

A change in heart and strategy would have been life-sustaining for our leads. Deceitful actions need to be made right. But Ananias and Sapphira had no such intentions. Instead, prestige took center stage in their lives. ✘

Take 3: Critic's Corner   (15 to 20 minutes)

Setup: Reinforce the points you want your students to take away from today's lesson.
Props: Group journal with entries from Take 1; **Outtakes** (p. 176); 2 buckets, 1
   beanbag, timer, marker

QUIET ON THE SET

Grab the group journal and ask students to review some of the "Gotcha!"
stories and the notes written during their Take 1 discussions.

ACTION

Consider the POV

Discuss some of the reasons middle schoolers are tempted to lie and the
consequences that result from lying. Ask the group:

- **What are the inner consequences of lying?**
- **We often lie to create a good impression or to look cool. How does lying to look good create a false ID?** *(When you lie, you're not being the person God means for you to be.)*
- **Pick an answer: Teen gossip is: a) nasty put-downs shot from a safe distance; b) half-truths, which make them OK; c) half-truths, which make them wrong; d) the only way to really know anything about anyone; e) a way to dish the dirt and get back at someone you don't like; f) all of the above. Explain your answer.**
- **Rumor control: How can you help put a stop to hurtful gossip?** *(No huddles with friends for the purpose of starting or spreading rumors.)*

Ask a volunteer to write "We Pledge . . . " in the group journal followed by a
group version of today's **Key Verse:** . . . "to keep [our] consciences clear before
God and man" (Acts 24:16). Have everybody sign the page.

Draw students' attention to the **POV** on **Outtakes** and repeat it together: *Lying to look good almost always backfires.*

Understand God's Truth

Number nine in God's Top Ten of commandments tells us this: Don't betray with lies. (See Exodus 20:16.) Instead, be kind to—and truthful with—those who live on this planet with you. Speak well of them and defend them. Choices made in truth cheer family and friends, classmates and peers.

Ask:

- **What have we learned from today's story?** *(Ananias and Sapphira lied to make themselves look good. They wanted recognition for something more than they actually gave.)*
- **What do you personally take away from this story?** *(The Christian life is not "every person for himself." We share a common life. What we do affects those around us.)*

You might say, *But people lie all the time!* Sadly, yes. But don't wait for the world to catch up to what you now know: Lies are a cheap imitation of truth. When you choose to live righteously, truth lives in you.

Teamwork

Are you a person who lives by the truth? Do others seek you out knowing that you can be trusted with their thoughts and feelings? Honesty empowers. Let's find creative ways to encourage each other to be spiritually healthy and honest this week.

PLAY BACK

Wrap up the meeting with a team-building activity that helps middle schoolers reflect on the importance of aiming for the truth at all times. Then close in prayer.

Lying in Wait

Needed: 2 buckets, 1 beanbag, timer, marker
Goal: Score points by aiming for "Truth."

How to Play:

Use the marker and print the word *Truth* on the buckets. Play this game like you would play basketball, substituting buckets for hoops and the beanbag for

Use a book, a shoe, a hefty rock, or something else to weigh down the buckets, preventing them from tipping over during the game.

Option: An idea to ease aggressive play: have more experienced team members play with their non-dominant hand only.

a ball. Set the buckets the length of "a court" apart (or, as far apart as possible in your room). Divide your group into two teams. Each team should have five to seven players on the "court." If you've got more than ten to fourteen students in all, have teams substitute players throughout the game.

Flip a coin to determine the starting team. Here's the fun part: The player holding the beanbag cannot move until he or she passes it—but his or her team can move. Players pass the beanbag toward the "Truth" buckets to score points. A score or missed shot at the bucket gives the opposing team a chance to play. Opposing players can block or intercept throws as they would in basketball, but stripping or stealing the beanbag is not allowed. The closest defender must be 3 to 5 feet out from their bucket. Play continues until time is called.

For competitive play, use a timer to keep playing time equal.

After the game, say: **The truth? Lies are ticking time bombs. Lies stink, bad. And almost all the time, someone else sniffs them out. Lies take the heart and soul out of really good people. Be a truth-teller and an honest friend instead. Trust God's Spirit to lead, guide, and give you expert direction.**

Close with Prayer

Verse-atility: *I will tell the truth and honor God and others.*

Ask your group to look again at **Outtakes** and repeat today's **Key Verse:** "I strive always to keep my conscience clear before God and man" (Acts 24:16). Then point out *Verse-atility*, a personalized rewording of today's Key Verse: *I will tell the truth and honor God and others.* Invite students to share prayer requests. Because of this week's topic, you might have them share in pairs or trios at most.

If the group prefers, have a silent prayer time this week. Here's a sample of a prayer starter you can lead for your students before allowing them to continue in silence: **"God, because you really know me, you know that I . . . (need help with/need help for/am scared about/would like advice on, etc.) ___ _____."**

End today's time by asking God to help each member of your class live out the main ideas of today's lesson. ✘

Gotcha!

Directions:

For some random word-game fun: fold your handout over and fill in the top portion before looking at the story below. Choose words that fit these descriptions and write them in the blanks. Any interesting word will do.

adjective: _____

proper noun: _____

noun: _____

verb ending in –ing: _____

body part: _____

liquid: _____

emotion: _____

animal: _____

digital device: _____

cartoon character: _____

geographical place: _____

adverb ending in -ly: _____

article of clothing: _____

number: _____

adverb ending in -ly: _____

animal (works best if same animal as used before): _____

color: _____

FOLD -

Gotcha!

Now put your words to use in this story. Fill in the blanks with the words you wrote above.

It was midnight on a night like no other when I heard a[n] _____(adjective) crash outside my bedroom window. I jumped. I knew it could only be _____ (proper noun). I tried to force my _____ (noun) out of bed, but I panicked and had trouble _____ (verb -ing). I ended up with my _____ (body part) in the _____ _____ (liquid).

When the slow, scratching noise on my door came, I was _____ (emotion). My older sister stuck her head in and groaned, "What did you do now?"

"It's all because of _____ (animal)," I cried. "He got into my _____ (digital device) and started going berserk like _____ (cartoon character)."

That didn't make a lot of sense, I know, but I couldn't tell her the truth or she would pack me off to _____ (geographical place).

As soon as she was gone, I bolted _____ (adverb -ly) to the window and peered out at the inky darkness.

What!? My _____ (article of clothing) was dangling in the tree and _____ (number) of my friends were cheering down below!

When the front door opened and my sis stepped out, my friends split _____ (adverb -ly).

"Somehow, I don't think this has anything to do with _____ (animal)," she muttered.

My mouth went dry. My face turned _____ (color). Caught!

Outtakes

CAST

Ananias: one of the earliest believers in Jesus
Sapphira: Ananias's wife
Peter: leader among the apostles, early leader in the Jerusalem church

MOVIE TRAILER

- The early Christians are dedicated to an attitude of generosity with each other.
- Ananias and Sapphira sell a field they own and keep part of the money.
- They give the rest of the money to the church leaders, but they say it's all of the money.
- Peter knows they're lying and confronts them.
- Because they lied to God, Ananias and Sapphira fall dead.

Verse-atility: I will tell the truth and honor God and others.

POV: Lying to look good almost always backfires.
Key Verse: "I strive always to keep my conscience clear before God and man" (Acts 24:16).

TO DIE FOR

Acts 4:32; 5:1-10 (The Message)
(We've added a few of our own comments in bold below.)

The whole congregation of believers was united as one—one heart, one mind! They didn't even claim ownership of their own possessions. No one said, "That's mine; you can't have it." They shared everything. . . .
    . . . But an **[audacious]** man named Ananias—his wife, Sapphira, conniving in this with him—sold a piece of land, secretly kept part of the price for himself, and then brought the rest to the apostles and made an offering of it.
    Peter **[a.k.a. the Lie Hunter]** said, "Ananias, how did Satan get you to lie to the Holy Spirit and secretly keep back part of the price of the field? Before you sold it, it was all yours, and after you sold it, the money was yours to do with as you wished. So what got into you to pull a trick like this? You didn't lie to men but to God."
    Ananias, when he heard those words, fell down **[no cliffhanger here]** dead. That put the fear of God into everyone who heard of it. The younger men went right to work and wrapped him up, then carried him out and buried him.
    Not more than three hours later, his wife, knowing nothing of what had happened, came in. Peter said, "Tell me, were you given this price for your field?"
    "Yes," she said, "that price." **[Bzzzz! Wrong answer.]**
    Peter responded, "What's going on here that you connived to conspire against the Spirit of the Master? The men who buried your husband are at the door, and you're next." No sooner were the words out of his mouth than she also fell down, dead. When the young men returned they found her body. They carried her out and buried her beside her husband.